HOCKEY
DRILL BOOK

Michael A. Smith

D0483346

*This book is dedicated to the memory of
my father, James Michael, who understood
the real value of youth hockey — participation.*

HOCKEY DRILL BOOK

Michael A. Smith

FIREFLY BOOKS

A FIREFLY BOOK

Published by Firefly Books Ltd. 2009

First printing

Publisher Cataloging-in-Publication Data (U.S.)
Smith, Michael A., 1945-
   Hockey drill book : 200 drills for player and team development / Michael A. Smith.
2nd ed.
[ ] p. : col. ill. ; cm.
Summary: A selection of drills that cover the fundamentals of: skating, stick handling,
passing, shooting, conditioning, goal tending, checking and game situations.
ISBN-13: 978-1-55407-552-2
ISBN-10: 1-55407-552-1
1. Hockey — Training. 2. Hockey – Coaching. I. Hockey drill book : two hundred
drills for player and team development. II. Title.
796.355 dc22   GV848.3.S658 2009

Library and Archives Canada Cataloguing in Publication
Smith, Michael A
   Hockey drill book : 200 drills for player and team
development / Michael A. Smith. — 2nd ed.
ISBN-13: 978-1-55407-552-2
ISBN-10: 1-55407-552-1
1. Hockey—Training. I. Title.
GV848 .3.S65 2009   796.962'2   C2009-900766-5

Published in the United States by
Firefly Books (U.S.) Inc.
P.O. Box 1338, Ellicott Station
Buffalo, New York 14205

Published in Canada by
Firefly Books Ltd.
66 Leek Crescent
Richmond Hill, Ontario L4B 1H1

Cover and interior design: Tinge Design Studio
Illustrations: Tinge Design Studio

Printed in China

The publisher gratefully acknowledges the financial support for our
publishing program by the Government of Canada through the Book Publishing
Industry Development Program.

CONTENTS

"Just give me a group of gentlemen, who play the game hard but clean, and always on an upward path. Then the championships will take care of themselves if the overall ability of the team warrants them."

John Wooden
They Call Me Coach

INTRODUCTION

The success of a hockey team, whether it is measured in individual skill improvement, winning, or fun, is directly dependent on practice. The better the practice, the better the team. What goes into a practice, how a practice is conducted and what is accomplished during a practice is critical. In this sense, the drills that a practice is comprised of are essential to the development of the team.

This book presents 200 drills in eight different chapters: skating, stickhandling, passing, shooting, conditioning, goaltending, checking and situations. The book presents a comprehensive selection of drills for the different levels of competition, and for different stages of development. The book is meant to serve all coaches, either as a readily available on-ice drill reminder, or as reference for new and different drills.

Each drill features: a full-color diagram, a purpose, a brief description, the number of participating players and the tempo of the drill's execution. All of this information is clearly displayed for quick reference. Many of the drills have variations listed as well.

No drill is too simple to be used. Drills are where the fundamental skills of the game are taught. All teams should constantly practice fundamentals and as a team develops its skills, the drills provided can be made more complex. Teams should, at some time, begin to use drills that combine multiple skills in one exercise.

The most important thing for the coach to consider when selecting a drill is that the drill should be fun: substantial, worthwhile and enjoyable. Good drills make coaching and playing a good experience.

KEY TO SYMBOLS

SYMBOL	DESCRIPTION
Ⓢ	Starting point
▲	Pylon
◄—	Skater; arrow shows direction of movement
- - -▶- - -	Skater with puck; arrow shows direction of movement
·····◄·····	Pass; arrow shows direction of movement
- -▶- -	Shot on goal; arrow shows direction of movement
⌒	Jump (over line or pylon)
✕✕✕✕✕✕	Skate backwards
✕✕✕✕✕✕✕	Stepovers
‖	Full stop

CHAPTER 1

Skating

"...the main thing in the tactics of this game was to be able to constantly create numerical superiority in every spot on the ice where the puck is, and in order to achieve this, they had to skate as they never skated before, wide open."

Anatoli Tarasov
Road to Olympus

Warm-up 1

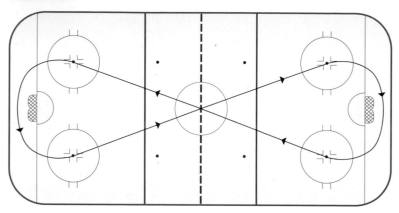

Purpose:
To provide a warm-up at the start of practice and to improve body movements while skating.

Description:
Performed while skating Figure 8's. A variety of body exercises are done to allow the players to stretch. The coach (or a player) can call out the exercises. Suggested exercises: knee bends, squats, body twists, run on toes, jumps, knee drops, full body drops, 180 and 360 degree spins.

Tempo:
Drill is started at a slow speed and increased during execution.

Participation:
The entire team.

Variations:
Performed while skating laps; performed in three groups, one group in each zone.

Warm-up 2

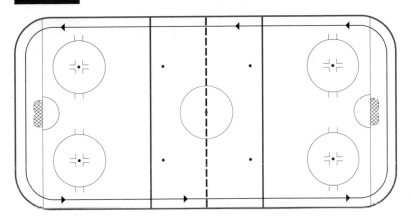

Purpose:

To provide a warm-up at the start of practice and to improve the player's dexterity with the stick.

Description:

Performed while skating laps. A variety of exercises focused on the stick are done to allow the players to stretch. The coach (or a player) can call out the exercises. Suggested exercises: rotate sticks with wrists, rotate at the hips with the stick behind the back, windmill type movement with stick behind the neck, touch the toes with both hands on the stick and bend forward touching the stick to the heels with stick behind the legs.

Tempo:

Drill is started at a slow speed and increased during execution.

Participation:

The entire team.

Variations:

Performed while skating Figure 8's; performed in three groups, one group in each zone.

Warm-up 3

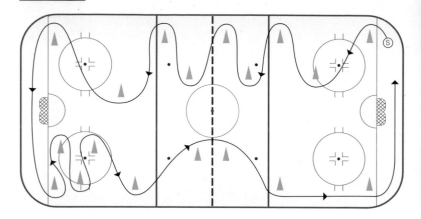

Purpose:

To provide a warm-up at the start of practice and to improve the player's skating ability.

Description:

Performed while skating laps. The players skate through a course laid out with obstacles. The obstacles are located to make the players execute short and long strides and tight and wide turns.

Tempo:

Drill is started at a slow speed and increased during execution.

Participation:

The entire team.

Variations:

Performed while skating backwards; performed alternating forward and backward skating; performed in time intervals, i.e., fast 10 seconds, slow 5 seconds; change the pattern of the obstacles.

Stops 1

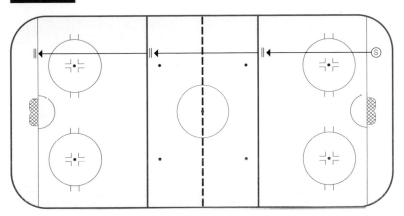

Purpose:

To provide a drill to practice stops.

Description:

Performed with players skating the length of the ice and stopping at the two blue lines and the far goal line. The drill should be repeated once the players reach the goal line. Players should face the same way when they stop to insure that stops on both sides are practiced.

Tempo:

Drill is executed from 3/4 to full speed.

Participation:

Team is divided into three or four groups. Drill is performed in groups. The second group starts after the first group has completed the first stop at the near blue line.

Variations:

Performed while skating backwards; performed alternating forward and backward skating.

Stops 2

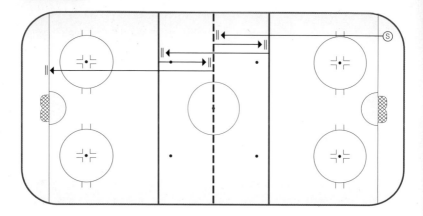

Purpose:

To provide a drill to practice stops and change of directions.

Description:

Players skate the length of ice in a predetermined pattern. One pattern is: to the red line, to the near blue line, to the far blue line, to the red line, to the far goal line. Players should face the same way when they stop to insure that stops on both sides are practiced.

Tempo:

Drill is executed from 3/4 to full speed.

Participation:

Team is divided into three or four groups. Drill is performed in groups. The second group starts after the first group has executed the second stop (near blue line).

Variations:

Performed while skating backwards; performed alternating forward and backward skating; performed with different patterns.

Stops 3

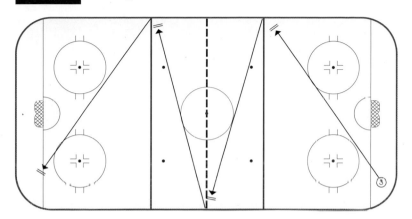

Purpose:
To provide a drill to practice stops and a change of directions.

Description:
Players skate a diagonal pattern stopping where the blue lines, red line and goal lines meet the boards. This is a good drill to practice one leg or partial stops. The players should face the same way when they stop to insure that stops on both sides are practiced.

Tempo:
Drill is executed from 3/4 to full speed.

Participation:
The entire team with one player right after another.

Variations:
Performed while skating backwards; performed alternating forward and backward skating; team is divided into two groups with each starting in opposite corners at the same end.

Stops 4

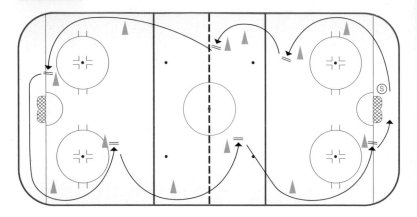

Purpose:

To provide a drill to practice stops while making turns.

Description:

Players skate in a course laid out with obstacles. The stops are executed at every second obstacle. The stops teach the players to stop during and after turns. The players should face the same way when stopping to insure that stops on both sides are executed.

Tempo:

Drill is executed from 3/4 to full speed.

Participation:

The entire team with one player right after another.

Variations:

Performed while skating backwards; performed alternating forward and backward skating; obstacles are changed to alter the pattern.

Stops 5

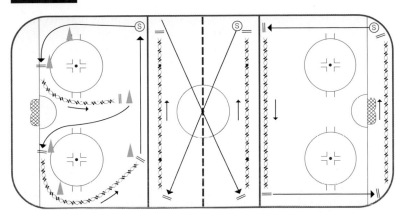

Purpose:

To provide a drill combining forward and backward stops.

Description:

Players skate in three different patterns, one in each zone. The drills teach the players to stop while skating forward and backward in different situations.

Tempo:

Drill is executed from 3/4 to full speed.

Participation:

Team is divided into three groups, one in each zone. The groups rotate through each zone.

Variations:

Change the patterns in each zone.

Stops 6

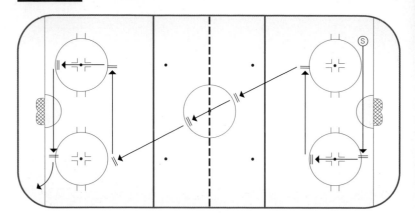

Purpose:

To provide a drill to practice stops.

Description:

Players skate in a predetermined pattern using the face-off circles. The pattern enables the players to practice stops while executing both long and short strides.

Tempo:

Drill is executed from 3/4 to full speed.

Participation:

The entire team with one player right after another.

Variations:

Change the pattern.

Stepovers 1

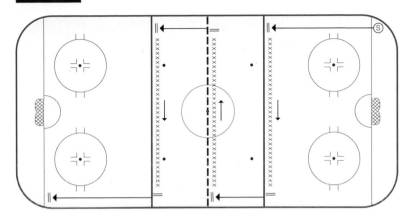

Purpose:

To provide a drill to practice stepovers.

Description:

Performed along the blue lines and red line. The coach must be sure the stepovers are executed properly. This is a good drill to find out which players have problems executing the stepovers. The players should always face the same end to insure that stepovers both ways are practiced.

Tempo:

Drill is executed at a normal speed relative to each group. If the drill is done too quickly, many players will not execute properly.

Participation:

The entire team with one player right after another.

Stepovers 2

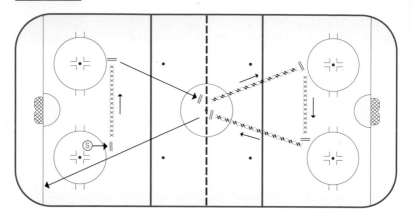

Purpose:

To provide a drill that combines stepovers with forward and backward skating.

Description:

Players execute stepovers, forward and backward skating in a predetermined pattern. This drill provides the opportunity to execute forward and backward turns as well. The coach must be sure the stepovers are executed properly.

Tempo:

Drill is executed at a normal speed relative to each group. If the drill is done too quickly, many players will not execute properly.

Participation:

The entire team with one player right after another.

Variations:

Change the pattern.

 ## DRILL 12 — Stepovers 3

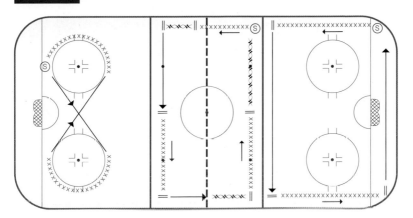

Purpose:
To provide a drill that combines stepovers with forward and backward skating.

Description:
Players execute stepovers in three different patterns, one in each zone. This drill combines forward and backward skating with stepovers. The coach must be sure the stepovers are executed properly.

Tempo:
Drill is executed at a normal speed relative to each group. If the drill is executed at a speed too quick, many players will not execute properly.

Participation:
The entire team is divided into three groups, one in each zone. The groups rotate through each zone.

Variations:
Change the patterns in each zone.

Crossovers 1

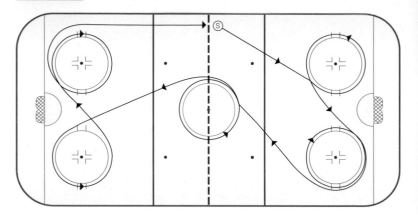

Purpose:

To provide a drill to practice crossovers.

Description:

Players skate around each of the five face-off circles. This enables the players to practice crossovers both to the left and to the right.

Tempo:

Drill is executed from 3/4 to full speed.

Participation:

Team is divided into groups of three to five players. The second group starts when the first group has completed its crossovers at the second face-off circle.

Variations:

Performed while skating backwards; performed alternating forward and backward skating.

Crossovers 2

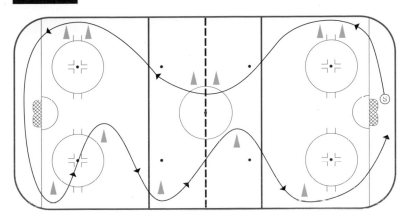

Purpose:

To provide a drill to practice crossovers.

Description:

Players skate in a predetermined pattern laid out with obstacles. The players practice both wide and tight crossovers.

Tempo:

Drill is executed from 3/4 to full speed.

Participation:

The entire team with one player right after another.

Variations:

Performed while skating backwards; performed alternating forward and backward skating; change the patterns.

DRILL 15

Crossovers 3

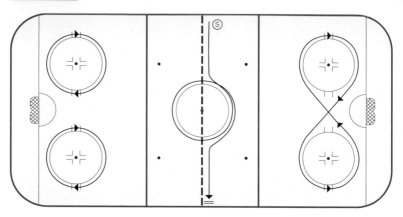

Purpose:
To provide a drill to practice crossovers.

Description:
Players skate three predetermined patterns, one in each zone. This drill emphasizes tight crossovers.

Tempo:
Drill is executed from 3/4 to full speed.

Participation:
Team is divided into three groups, one to each zone. The groups rotate through each zone.

Variations:
Performed while skating backwards; performed alternating forward and backward skating.

Crossovers 4

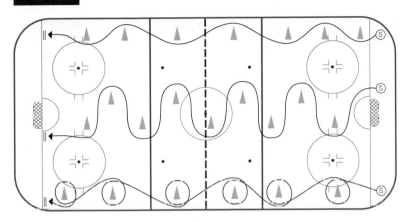

Purpose:
To provide a drill to practice crossovers.

Description:
Players skate three predetermined patterns laid out with obstacles. The patterns allow wide and tight crossovers to be executed.

Tempo:
Drill is executed from 3/4 to full speed.

Participation:
Team is divided into three groups, one for each pattern. The groups rotate through each pattern.

Variations:
Performed while skating backwards; change the patterns.

Stops and Crossovers 1

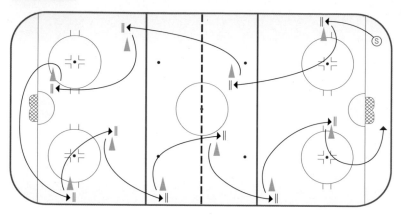

Purpose:

To provide a drill that combines stops and crossovers.

Description:

Players skate in a pattern laid out with obstacles. The players execute crossovers both to the left and right. The crossovers are executed after the stops.

Tempo:

Drill is executed from 3/4 to full speed.

Participation:

The entire team with one player right after another.

Variations:

Performed while skating backwards; performed alternating forward and backward skating; change the pattern.

Stops and Crossovers 2

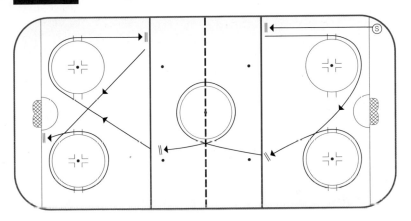

Purpose:
To provide a drill that combines stops and crossovers.

Description:
Players skate in a pattern that is laid out with the face-off circles. The players execute crossovers and stops both to the left and right.

Tempo:
Drill is executed from 3/4 to full speed.

Participation:
The entire team with one player right after another.

Variations:
Performed while skating backwards; performed alternating forward and backward skating.

Balance 1

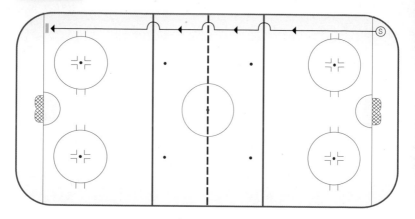

Purpose:
To provide a drill to practice jumps.

Description:
Players skate length of ice executing jumps at the blue lines and the red line.

Tempo:
Drill is executed at a normal speed relative to each group. If the drill is executed at a speed too quick, many players will not execute the jumps properly.

Participation:
Team is divided into groups of three to five players. The second group starts when the first group has completed its first jump.

Variations:
Performed while skating backwards.

Balance 2

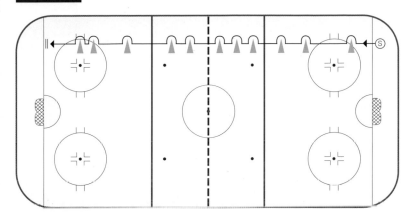

Purpose:

To provide a drill to practice jumps.

Description:

Players skate length of ice executing jumps over the obstacles. The obstacles are laid in a manner that enables the players to jump from both short and long strides.

Tempo:

Drill is executed at a normal speed relative to each group. If the drill is executed at a speed too quick, many players will not execute the jumps properly.

Participation:

The entire team with one player right after another.

Variations:

Change the pattern.

Balance 3

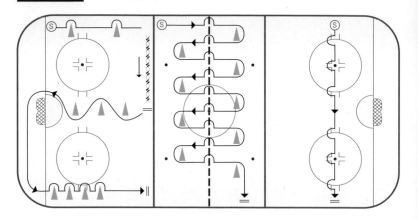

Purpose:

To provide a drill to practice jumps.

Description:

The players skate three patterns, one in each zone. This drill combines crossovers, forward and backward skating and jumps.

Tempo:

Drill is executed at a normal speed relative to each group. If the drill is executed at a speed too quick, many players will not execute the jumps properly.

Participation:

Team is divided into three groups, one in each zone. The groups rotate through each zone.

Variations:

Change the patterns in each zone.

Balance 4

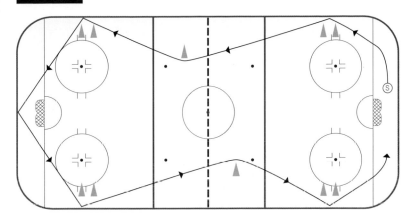

Purpose:

To provide a drill that teaches the players to maintain their balance after contact with the boards.

Description:

Performed while skating laps. The players make contact at the designated spots. This is executed in a manner that has the player throwing thier body against the boards while skating.

Tempo:

Drill is executed at a normal speed relative to each group. If the drill is executed at a speed too quick, the players will not maintain their balance after the contact.

Participation:

The entire team with one player right after another.

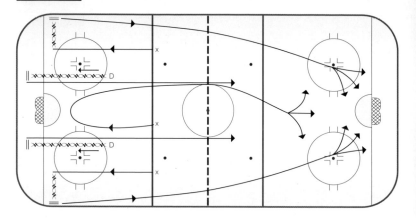

Purpose:

To provide a drill that simulates the skating patterns of the team's breakout system.

Description:

The players execute the positional skating patterns of the team's breakout system. The players should interchange with the different positions to be familiar with the different patterns.

Tempo:

Drill is executed from 3/4 to full speed.

Participation:

Team is divided into five-player units. Drill can also be executed with just the forwards or defensemen.

Defensive System

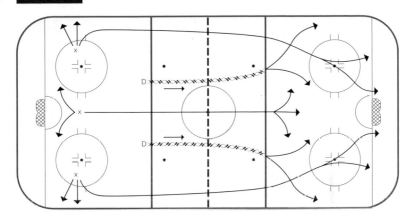

Purpose:

To provide a drill that simulates the skating patterns of the team's defensive system.

Description:

The players execute the positional skating patterns of the team's defensive system. The players should interchange with the different positions to be familiar with the different patterns.

Tempo:

Drill is executed from 3/4 to full speed.

Participation:

Team is divided into five player units. Drill can also be performed with just the forwards or defensemen

Obstacle Course

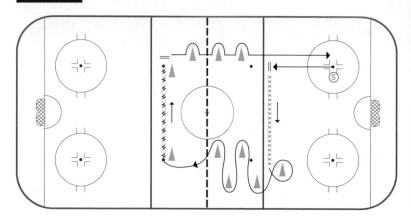

Purpose:

To provide a drill that practices the different skating skills.

Description:

An obstacle course is laid out. The players skate the course executing the different skills. It should include forward and backward skating, crossovers, stepovers, jumps and stops.

Tempo:

Drill is executed at full speed.

Participation:

The entire team. Drill may be executed one at a time or one player right after another.

Variations:

Change the course; time participants.

CHAPTER 2

Stickhandling

"When learning a movement, keep to the principle of going from the 'known to unknown', then you are sure to make progress."

Oleg Spassky
Ice Hockey

Warm-up 1

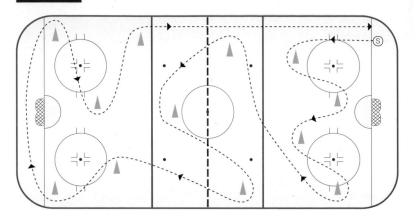

Purpose:

To provide a warm-up at the start of practice and to improve the player's ability to handle the puck.

Description:

Performed with the players skating a pattern laid out with obstacles. The pattern is such that the players make tight and wide turns while carrying the puck.

Tempo:

Drill is started at a slow speed and increased during execution.

Participation:

The entire team with one player right after another.

Variations:

Performed while skating backwards; change the pattern.

Warm-up 2

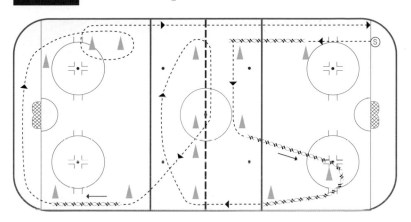

Purpose:

To provide a warm-up at the start of practice and to improve the player's ability to handle the puck.

Description:

Performed with the players skating a pattern laid out with obstacles. The pattern is such that the players work on the transition between forward and backward skating while handling the puck.

Tempo:

Drill is started at a slow speed and increased slightly during execution.

Participation:

The entire team with one player right after another.

Variations:

Change the pattern; include stepovers by inserting them into a segment.

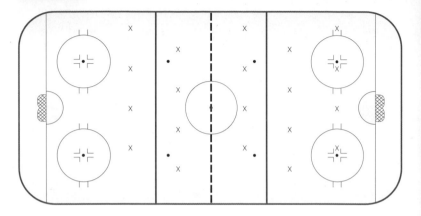

Purpose:

To provide a drill to practice the fundamentals of puckhandling.

Description:

Players are spread out over the ice. Start with the players stationary. Practice the basic fundamentals: regular dribble, short dribble, wide dribble, and quick dribble. Next, have the players make short movements (2–3 strides) to the left, right, forward and backward. Dekes (against invisible opponents) should be practiced. Other things, such as dropping to one knee and both knees while stickhandling, can also be practiced.

Tempo:

Stationary, the movements begin at a slow speed and gradually increase.

Participation:

The entire team.

Puckhandling and Turns 1

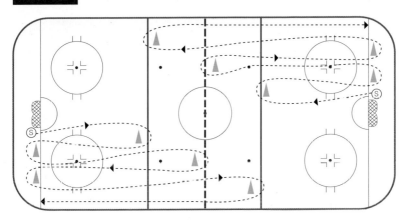

Purpose:

To provide a drill to practice turns while handling the puck.

Description:

Players skate forward to the near blue line, make a turn and return to the goal line. This is repeated to the red line and the far blue line. Obstacles are used for the turns.

Tempo:

Drill is executed from 3/4 to full speed.

Participation:

Team is divided into two groups, one at each end of the ice. The second player starts when the first reaches the near blue line.

Variations:

Performed skating backwards.

DRILL
30   Puckhandling and Turns 2

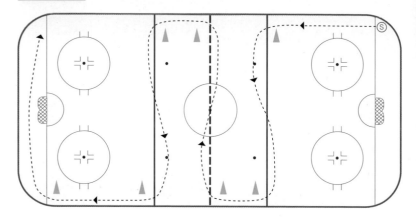

Purpose:

To provide a drill to practice turns while handling the puck.

Description:

Performed by skating along the two blue lines and the red lines. Obstacles are used as guides.

Tempo:

Drill is executed from 3/4 to full speed.

Participation:

The entire team with one player right after another.

Variations:

Performed skating backwards.

Puckhandling and Turns 3

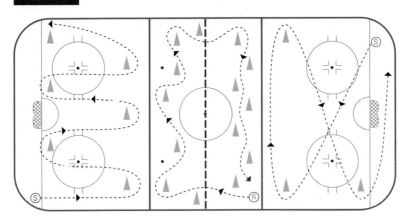

Purpose:

To provide a drill to practice turns while handling the puck.

Description:

Players skate in three different patterns, one in each zone. The patterns are laid out with obstacles. The patterns are such that both wide and tight turns are executed.

Tempo:

Drill is executed from 3/4 to full speed.

Participation:

Team is divided into three groups, one in each zone. The groups rotate through each zone.

Variations:

Performed while skating backwards; performed alternating forward and backward skating.

Puckhandling and Turns 4

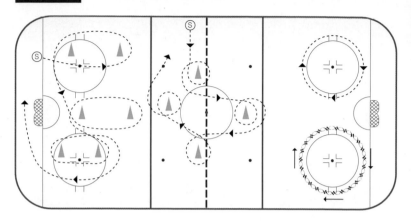

Purpose:

To provide a drill to practice crossovers while handling the puck.

Description:

Players skate three different patterns, one in each zone. The patterns are laid out with obstacles and the face-off circles. The patterns are such that both wide and tight crossovers are executed.

Tempo:

Drill is executed from 1/2 to full speed.

Participation:

Team is divided into three groups, one in each zone. The groups rotate through each zone.

Variations:

Performed while skating backwards; performed alternating forward and backward skating; change the patterns.

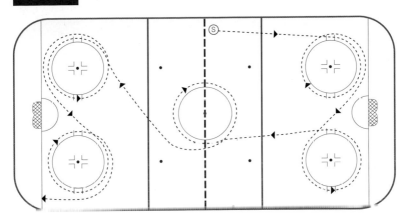

Purpose:
To provide a drill to practice crossovers while handling the puck.

Description:
Players skate around each of the five face-off circles. This enables the players to practice crossovers to the left and right while handling the puck.

Tempo:
Drill is executed from 3/4 to full speed.

Participation:
Team is divided into groups of three to five players. The second group starts when the first group has completed its crossovers at the second face-off circle.

Variations:
Performed while skating backwards; performed alternating forward and backward skating.

Puckhandling and Circles 2

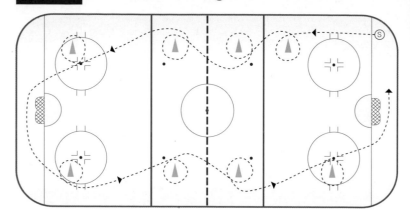

Purpose:

To provide a drill to practice crossovers while handling the puck.

Description:

Obstacles are laid out around the rink in a lap like fashion. Players skate around the rink executing tight circles around each of the obstacles.

Tempo:

Drill is executed from 1/2 to full speed.

Participation:

The entire team; the second player leaves after the first player has completed the first circle.

Variations:

Performed while skating backwards; performed alternating forward and backward skating; the number of obstacles can be increased or decreased.

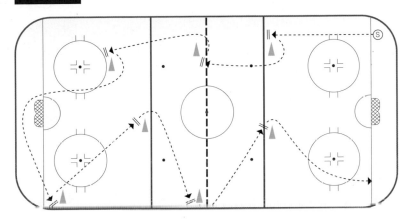

Purpose:

To provide a drill to practice stops while handling the puck.

Description:

Players skate a predetermined pattern laid out with obstacles. Full stops are executed at each obstacle. The coach must be sure players practice stops both ways.

Tempo:

Drill is executed from 3/4 to full speed.

Participation:

The entire team; the second player leaves after the first player has completed his first stop.

Variations:

Change the pattern.

Puckhandling and Stops 2

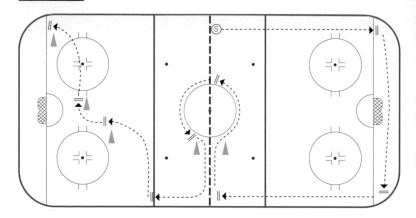

Purpose:

To provide a drill to practice stops while handling the puck.

Description:

Players skate a predetermined pattern laid out with obstacles, face-off circles and the blue and red lines. Drill enables players to execute stops while handling the puck on a straight line, while making crossovers and while making turns.

Tempo:

Drill is executed from 3/4 to full speed.

Participation:

The entire team; the second player leaves after the first player has completed the first stop.

Variations:

Change the pattern.

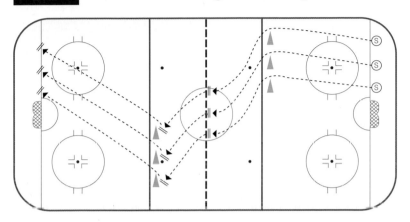

Purpose:

To provide a drill to practice stops while handling the puck.

Description:

Players skate the length of the ice executing turns and stops at the blue and red lines. Obstacles may be used.

Tempo:

Drill is executed at full speed.

Participation:

The team is divided into groups of three. The second group leaves after the first group passes the near blue line.

Variations:

Change the pattern.

Puckhandling Medley

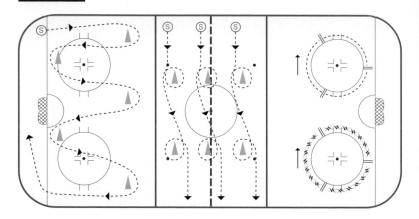

Purpose:

To provide a drill to practice various skating skills while handling the puck.

Description:

Players skate three different patterns, one in each zone. The patterns are laid out with the face-off circles and obstacles. Any number of skills can be practiced. In this example, turns, crossovers and stops are used.

Tempo:

Drill is executed from 3/4 to full speed.

Participation:

Team is divided into three groups, one in each zone. The groups rotate through each zone.

Variations:

Performed skating backwards; performed alternating forward and backward skating; change the patterns; change the skating skills.

Chaos 1

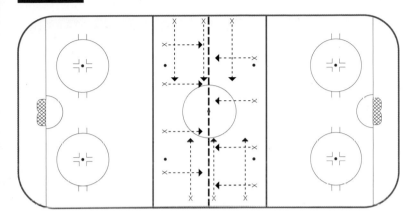

Purpose:

To provide a drill to train players to keep their heads up, maintain body control and control the puck.

Description:

Players are divided into four groups. Two are lined up on opposite blue lines, and the other two are lined up on opposite boards at neutral ice. The groups skate simultaneously to the opposite side, with heads up and handling the puck. Players try to avoid contact while controlling the puck.

Tempo:

Drill is executed at 1/2 speed. To execute at a quicker tempo depends on the skill level of the players.

Participation:

The entire team, each group can hold up to six to seven players.

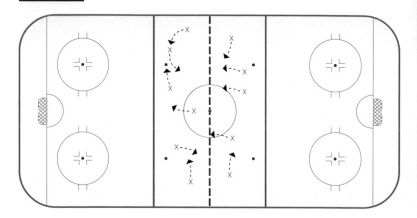

Purpose:
To provide a drill to train players to keep their heads up, maintain body control and control the puck.

Description:
Players are confined to a limited area; in this drill, the neutral zone. Each player has a puck. The players skate in all directions avoiding contact while handling the puck.

Tempo:
Drill is executed at 1/2 speed. To execute at a quicker tempo depends on the skill level of the players.

Participation:
The entire team. If smaller areas are used, fewer players may be used.

Variations:
Change the area size; insert a small number of players without a puck to try to knock the pucks away from the other players.

Chaos 3

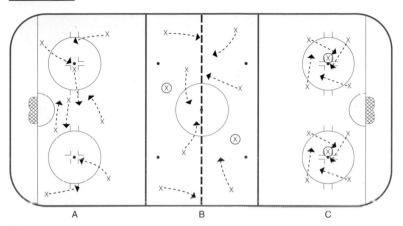

A	B	C

Purpose:

To provide a drill to train players to keep their heads up, maintain body control and control the puck.

Description:

Three different drills are executed, one in each zone. The drills are: (A) everyone with a puck; (B) a few players ⊗ without pucks attempting to steal the pucks from the others; (C) one player ⊗ in face-off circle attempting to steal the puck from the others.

Tempo:

Drill is executed at 1/2 speed. To execute at a quicker tempo depends on the skill level of the players.

Participation:

Team is divided into three groups, one in each zone. The groups rotate through each zone.

Chaos 4

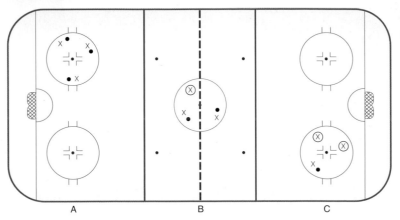

A   B   C

Purpose:

To provide a drill to train players to keep their heads up, maintain body control and control the puck.

Description:

Three different drills are executed using the face-off circles. The drills are: (A) each player has a puck and they move in different directions; (B) two players have pucks and one ⊗ player does not. The player without the puck attempts to steal the pucks from the others; (C) one player has a puck and two players ⊗ are without pucks. The players without pucks attempt to steal the puck from the other.

Tempo:

Drill is executed at 3/4 to full speed.

Participation:

Team is divided into groups of three. One group is assigned to each circle.

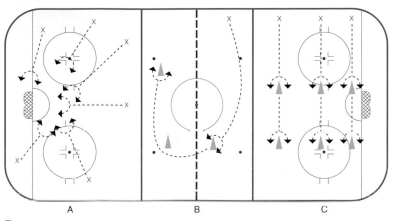

A   B   C

Purpose:

To provide a drill for the players with pucks to practice beating players without pucks (dekes).

Description:

Three different drills are executed, one in each zone. The drills are: (A) players move toward the net making dekes; (B) players make dekes at stationary objects; (C) players make dekes at stationary objects.

Tempo:

Drill is executed from 1/2 to full speed.

Participation:

Team is divided into three groups, one in each zone. The groups rotate through each zone.

Variations:

Insert players without pucks to contest the players with the pucks.

2-0/1-1

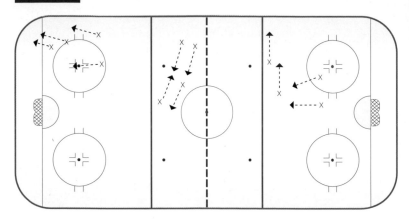

Purpose:

To provide a drill that makes puckhandling and dekeing competitive.

Description:

Players skate in pairs, each pair in a different direction with one puck per pair. At time intervals, players will skate 2–0 with one player handling the puck, then 1–1 with players contesting for control of the puck. Note: this is a good conditioning drill. For example, 10 seconds 2–0, 10 seconds 1–1, and 10 seconds rest.

Tempo:

Drill is executed at full speed.

Participation:

The entire team.

Variations:

Players can pass the puck during the 2–0 segment.

Retrieve Pucks 1

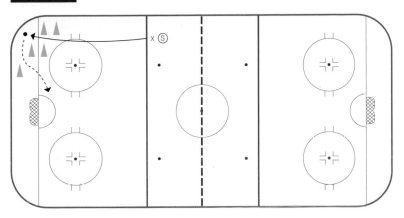

Purpose:

To provide a drill to teach players to gain control of the puck and carry it from the corner.

Description:

Obstacles are placed in the corner. A player will skate into the corner, gain control of the puck and move from the corner. The obstacles force the player to execute skating skills while moving from the corner.

Tempo:

Drill is executed from 3/4 to full speed.

Participation:

Team can be divided up into as many as four groups, one to each corner.

Variations:

See Chapter 7 for checking drills.

46 Retrieve Pucks 2

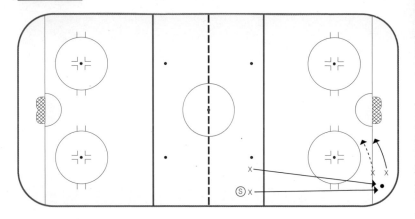

Purpose:

To provide a drill to teach players to gain control of the puck and carry it from the corner.

Description:

Two players race to the corner. The first player takes control of the puck and must beat the second player to reach the net.

Tempo:

Drill is executed at full speed.

Participation:

Team can be divided up into as many as four groups, one to each corner.

Variations:

See Chapter 7 for checking drills.

Retrieve Pucks 3

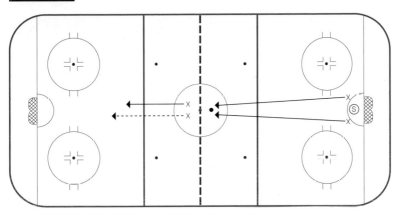

Purpose:

To provide a game type competitive drill.

Description:

Two players race for a puck that is at center ice. The first player to the puck continues toward the net, and the second player attempts to prevent the first from getting there.

Tempo:

Drill is executed at full speed.

Participation:

The entire team, usually the winners continue to compete until there is a final winner.

Puckhandling and the Feet 1

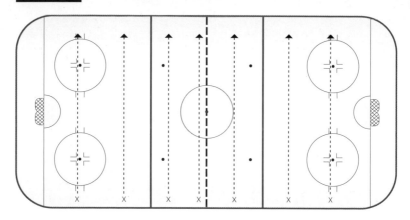

Purpose:

To teach players to control the puck with their feet.

Description:

Players, without sticks, skate across the ice and control the puck with their feet.

Tempo:

Drill is executed at 1/2 speed. To execute at a quicker tempo depends on the skill level of the players.

Participation:

The entire team.

Puckhandling and the Feet 2

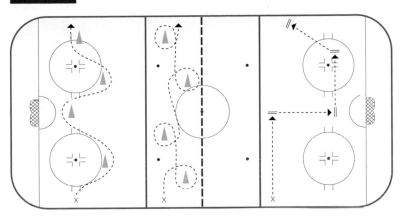

Purpose:
To teach players to control the puck with their feet.

Description:
Three different patterns are laid out. The players execute each pattern by carrying the puck with their feet.

Tempo:
Drill is executed at 1/2 speed. To execute at a quicker tempo depends on the skill level of the players.

Participation:
The team is divided into three groups, one in each zone.

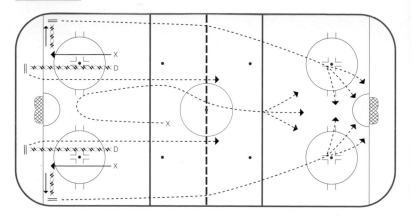

Purpose:

To provide a drill that simulates the puckhandling patterns of the team's breakout system.

Description:

The players execute the positional puckhandling patterns of the team's breakout system. Practice the players getting the puck at different places in the pattern. The players should interchange with the different positions to be familiar with the different patterns.

Tempo:

Drill is executed from 3/4 to full speed.

Participation:

Team is divided into five-player units. Drill can also be executed with just the forwards or the defensemen.

CHAPTER 3

Passing

"In order to receive or pass the puck in time, you must be well oriented in the play situation, see everything happening on the ice to foresee the immediate developments of the game... Try to control the puck — not with your eyes, but with your stick. Keep your head high, watch your teammates and everything that is happening around you. And smile, make sure you smile. It is easier to master most intricate elements with a smile."

Nikolai Golomazov
Ice Hockey

Stationary Passing

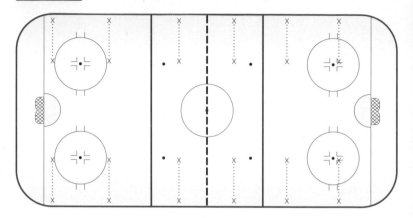

Purpose:

To provide a drill to practice the fundamentals of passing.

Description:

Players are spread out over the ice in pairs. Start with the players stationary. Practice the basic passes: wrist, snap, slap, lift and backhand. Have the players take the passes on the forehand, backhand and facing each other. Also vary the distances.

Tempo:

Begin with slow and easy passes and progress gradually to crisp passes.

Participation:

The entire team.

Passes Making Laps

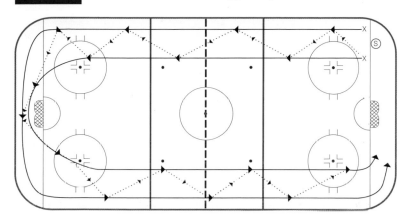

Purpose:

To provide a warm-up at the start of practice that utilizes passes.

Description:

Performed while skating laps. Players skate in pairs executing passes.

Tempo:

Drill is started at a slow speed and is increased during execution.

Participation:

The entire team.

Variations:

Players skate up the middle and turn, as a pair, to either side.

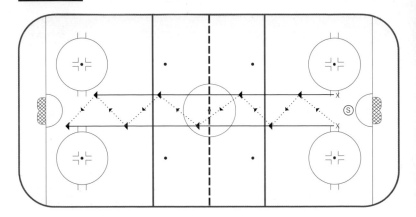

Purpose:

To provide a drill to teach short passes and one-touch passes.

Description:

Players skate up the middle as a pair making short passes. Begin the drill with the players taking the pass and making a return pass after a couple of strides. Progress to one-touch passing: receiving the pass and making the return pass are executed simultaneously.

Tempo:

Drill is started at a slow speed and is increased as the passing skill is improved.

Participation:

The entire team.

Variations:

Pairs go down the middle and back one side; pairs go down the middle and split up with one player coming back on each side.

Short Passes 2

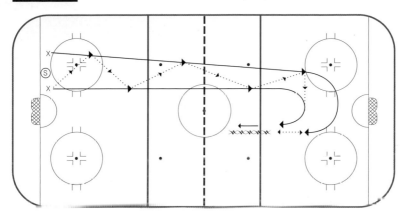

Purpose:

To provide a drill to teach short passes and one-touch passes.

Description:

Players skate up the middle as a pair making short passes. The players come back with one skating backward and one skating forward making one-touch passes.

Tempo:

Drill is started at a slow speed and is increased as the passing skill is improved.

Participation:

The entire team.

Short Passes 3

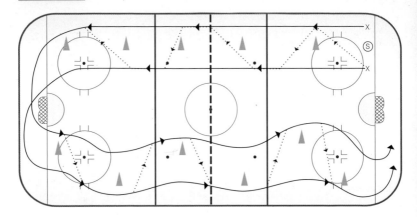

Purpose:

To provide a drill to teach short passes and one-touch passes.

Description:

Obstacles are laid out along each side of the ice. Players skate laps in pairs passing between the obstacles. The players can either go in straight lines or in a weave pattern. Progress to one-touch passes.

Tempo:

Drill is started at a slow speed and is increased as the passing skill is improved.

Participation:

The entire team.

Short Passes 4

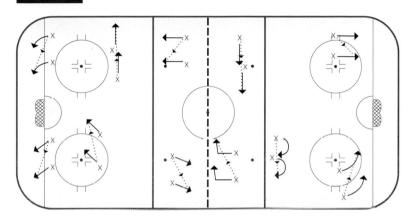

Purpose:

To provide a drill to teach short passes and one-touch passes.

Description:

Players are spread around the ice in pairs. As pairs, players move in a confined area in all directions. Short- and one-touch passes are executed. This drill teaches anticipation.

Tempo:

Drill is executed from 3/4 to full speed.

Participation:

The entire team.

Short Passes 5

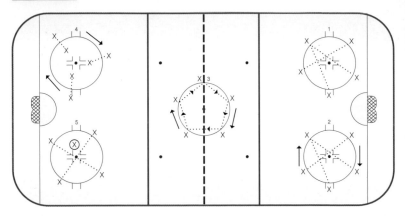

Purpose:

To provide a drill to teach short passes and one-touch passes.

Description:

Five different drills are executed, one in each face-off circle. (1) Stationary diagonal passes; (2) diagonal passes while moving; (3) pass to player in front while moving; (4) players skating in pairs around face-off circle; (5) man in middle ⊗ tries to intercept diagonal passes.

Tempo:

Drill is executed from 3/4 to full speed.

Participation:

Team is divided into five groups, one in each face-off circle.

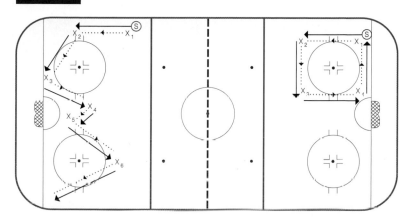

Purpose:

To provide a drill to teach short passes and one-touch passes with player movement.

Description:

Players are aligned in groups of four to six. A player makes a pass and then follows the puck to that player. For example, X_1 passes to X_2 and X_1 moves to where X_2 is. X_2 passes to X_3 and moves to where X_3 is.

Tempo:

Drill is executed from 3/4 to full speed.

Participation:

Team is divided into groups. The number and size of groups can vary. It is best to start with small groups and have the player movement be short. Increase the size of the group and distance as the passing skills improve.

Short Passes 7

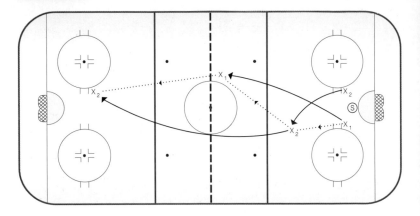

Purpose:

To provide a drill to teach short passes and one-touch passes.

Description:

The drill teaches players, working in pairs, to head man the puck with short passes. The player making the pass breaks for an open spot for a return pass. For example, X_2 moves ahead of X_1 for a pass, X_1 moves ahead of X_2 for a pass and so on.

Tempo:

Drill is started at a slow speed and is increased as the passing skill is improved.

Participation:

The entire team.

Short Passes 8

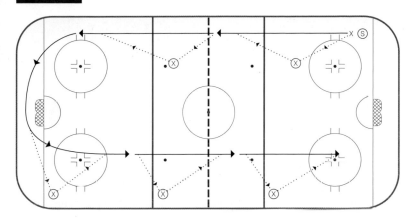

Purpose:

To provide a drill to teach short passes and one touch passes.

Description:

Players (X) skate around the ice in laps passing to other players ⊗ who make return passes to X. Drill should progress until both X and ⊗ make one-touch passes.

Tempo:

Drill is executed from 3/4 to full speed.

Participation:

The entire team; the second player leaves after first player makes his initial pass.

Variations:

Obstacles can be inserted to increase the difficulty.

Long Passes 1

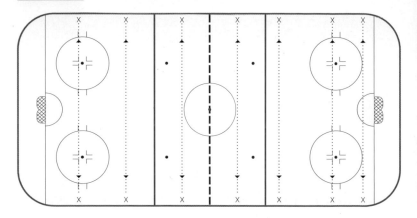

Purpose:

To provide a drill to teach long passes.

Description:

Players are lined up along the boards. Working in pairs, the basic fundamentals of long passes are practiced. Emphasis is placed on the wrist pass.

Tempo:

Begin with slow easy passes and progress to crisp passes.

Participation:

The entire team.

Variations:

Players can work in groups of four and receive the pass from one player and pass to another.

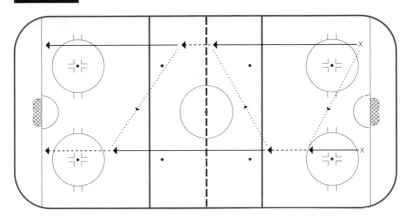

Purpose:

To provide a drill to teach long passes with player movement.

Description:

Players, working in pairs, skate the length of the ice. Each player stays wide to make the long passes.

Tempo:

Drill is started at a slow speed and is increased as the passing skill is improved.

Participation:

The entire team; the second pair starts after first pair completes initial pass.

Variations:

Each player, skating up the ice, moves toward the middle after making the pass and returns toward the boards after receiving the pass. This results in a weave pattern.

Long Passes 3

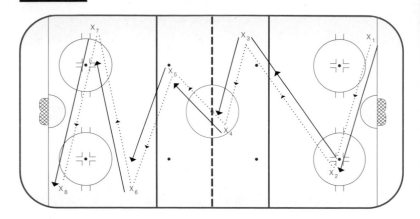

Purpose:
To provide a drill to teach long passes and player movement.

Description:
Players are lined up along the ice in a pattern which keeps long distances between players. A player makes the pass to the next player and follows the puck to that player. For example, X_1 passes to X_2 and moves to where X_2 is. X_2 passes to X_3 and moves to where X_3 is.

Tempo:
Drill is executed from the 3/4 to full speed.

Participation:
The entire team. Team can be divided into groups of a few players (4–6).

Variations:
The number of players can change.

"Move the Puck"

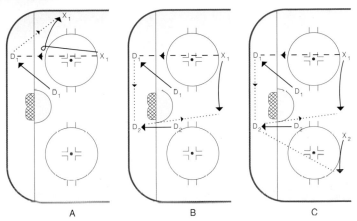

A   B   C

Purpose:
To provide a drill to teach defensemen to move the puck quickly in their own end.

Description:
Two players, a forward (X_1) and a defenseman (D_1), perform the basic drill (A). X_1 dumps the puck in the corner, and D_1 moves to the corner. D_1 moves the puck quickly to X_1 who has moved to the boards.

Tempo:
Drill is executed at full speed.

Participation:
Drill can be practiced at both ends of the ice or only one end.

Variations:
Players can be added for more complete defensive zone work (B & C).

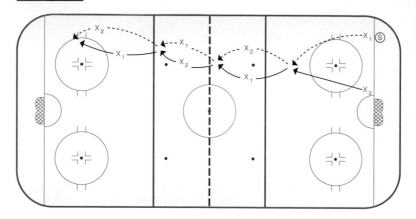

Purpose:

To provide a drill to teach the drop pass.

Description:

X_1 skates with the puck, X_2 comes from behind and X_1 drop passes to X_2. X_2 proceeds with the puck and X_1 slows down and then comes from behind for a drop pass from X_2. Drill is executed around the rink.

Tempo:

Drill is started at a slow speed and is increased as the passing skill is improved.

Participation:

The entire team; the second pair starts after first pair clears the near blue line.

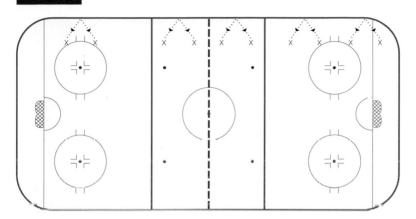

Purpose:

To provide a drill to teach the use of the boards while passing.

Description:

Players are spread around the ice and work in pairs. The players direct the passes to each other by banking the puck off the boards. Players should make passes both on the forehand and the backhand as well as receive passes the same way.

Tempo:

Drill is started with slow easy passes and progresses to crisp quick passes.

Participation:

The entire team.

Variations:

The player makes short movements.

Board Pass 2

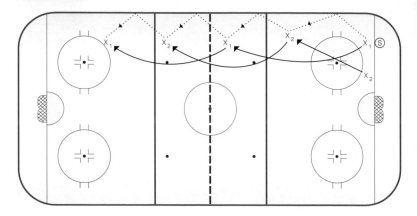

Purpose:

To provide a drill to teach the use of boards while passing to a moving player.

Description:

Players work in pairs and move around the ice in a lap like fashion. In this drill, one player is stationary and one is moving. X_1 is stationary and passes off of the boards to X_2 who is moving to receive the pass. X_1 then moves ahead of X_2 (who is stationary) to receive a board pass.

Tempo:

Drill is executed at a slow speed and is increased as the passing skill is improved.

Participation:

The entire team.

Board Pass 3

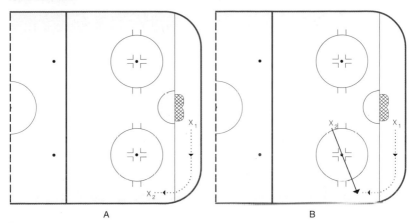

A   B

Purpose:

To provide a drill to teach the use of the board pass to clear the defensive zone.

Description:

In this drill, X_1 passes to X_2 who is on the boards (A). This drill teaches both the art of passing along the boards and of receiving a board pass. Drill should progress to a point that X_2 can move to the boards and simultaneously receive the pass (B).

Tempo:

Drill is executed at a slow speed and is increased as the passing skill is improved.

Participation:

The entire team. Drill can be executed in the four corners.

Back Pass 1

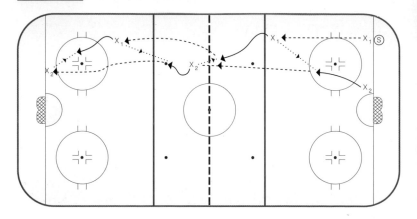

Purpose:
To provide a drill to teach the back pass.

Description:
Performed with two players as a pair. X_1, with a puck, moves ahead of X_2 and makes a back pass to X_2. X_2 then moves ahead of X_1 and makes a back pass to X_1.

Tempo:
Drill is executed at a slow speed and is increased as the passing skill is improved.

Participation:
The entire team.

Variations:
Have a third player join the pair and the three work the drill as a unit.

Back Pass 2

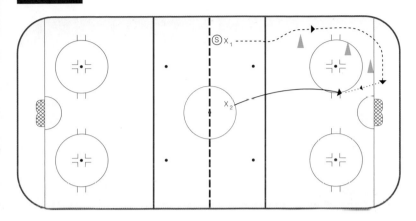

Purpose:

To provide a drill to teach the back pass in the slot area.

Description:

Performed with two players; one moving toward the net and the other along the boards. The first player, X_1, carries the puck deep behind the goal line. The second player, X_2, moves toward the slot area. X_1 makes a back pass to X_2 in the slot area.

Tempo:

Drill is executed from 3/4 to full speed.

Participation:

Team is divided into four groups, two in each end.

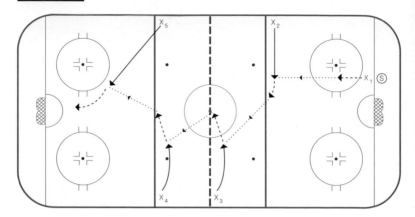

Purpose:

To provide a drill to teach quick puck advancement to the "head man."

Description:

Players are grouped (X_1 to X_5) at different spots on the ice. The puck is moved quickly to the next player who is skating ahead to force the pass. This is a quick tempo drill, and the head man must be moving to force the quick head pass. X_1 passes to X_2 and moves to X_2's spot, X_2 to X_3 and so on.

Tempo:

Drill is executed from 3/4 to full speed.

Participation:

The entire team. Team can be divided into groups (4–8).

Variations:

Change the number of groups to dictate long and short passes; groups align themselves at different places on the ice.

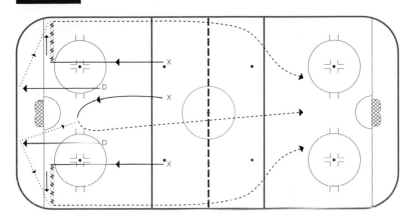

Purpose:

To provide a drill that simulates the passing patterns of the team's breakout system.

Description:

The players execute the positional passing patterns of the team's breakout system. Practice the players receiving the passes at different places in the patterns. The players should interchange with the different positions to be familiar with the different patterns.

Tempo:

Drill is executed from 3/4 to full speed.

Participation:

Team is divided into five-player units. Drill can also be executed with just the forwards or the defensemen.

Offensive Zone Passing

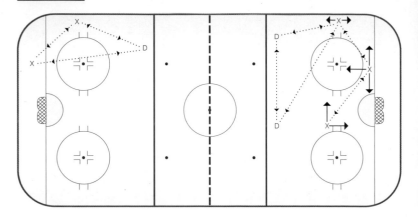

Purpose:

To provide a drill to teach the passing patterns in the offensive zone.

Description:

The players pass the puck around in the offensive zone. This drill enables work to be made for specific situations. The drill teaches offensive anticipation and movement as a total unit.

Tempo:

Drill is executed at full speed.

Participation:

Team is divided into five-player units and can be executed at both ends.

Variations:

Fewer players can be used to work on specific plays.

Passing Game

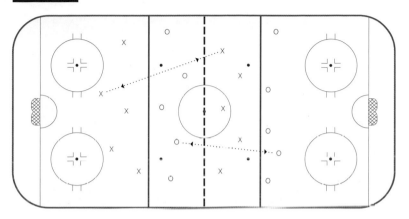

Purpose:

To provide a competitive drill to utilize passing skills.

Description:

Two teams, X's and O's, are aligned as in the diagram. The X's attempt to keep the puck while passing back and forth between the two groups of X's. The O's attempt to gain control of the puck and keep it from the X's.

Tempo:

Players will dictate the tempo, usually full speed.

Participation:

The entire team, divided into two teams.

Variations:

Add additional pucks but not too many. Three is usually the limit.

Relay Races

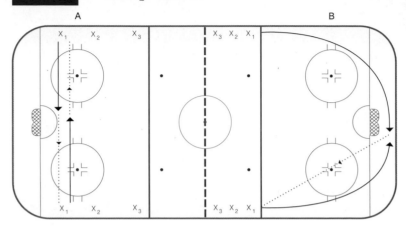

Purpose:

To provide a competitive drill to utilize passing skills.

Description:

Team is divided into groups and competitive passing games are played: (A) players skate to the middle and pass to a group member on the opposite board; (B) players skate behind the net and pass to a group member at the red line.

Tempo:

Drill is executed at full speed.

Participation:

The entire team. Team is divided into groups. Normally, the groups should have 4–8 players.

CHAPTER 4

Shooting

"Home is the sailor, home from sea,

And the hunter home from the hill. "

Robert Louis Stevenson
Requiem

Stationary Shooting

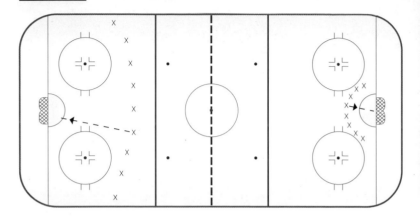

Purpose:

To provide a warm-up shooting drill.

Description:

Performed with the players stationary and shooting from that position. Distances can be varied, i.e., from the blue line, half-way between the net and blue line, close to the net. Practice the different shots: wrist, snap, backhand and slap.

Tempo:

Drill is executed from 3/4 to full speed.

Participation:

The entire team, half at each end.

Variations:

Players take a couple strides before shooting; players take a pass from the corner before shooting; players shoot 2–3 pucks at a time.

Swing-out

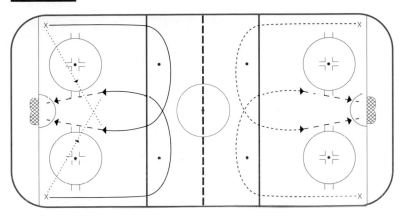

Purpose:
To provide a warm-up shooting drill while skating.

Description:
Performed with players rotating out of the corners. Players skate from the corner past the blue line and swing in toward the net. Practice the different shots and vary the distances.

Tempo:
Drill is executed from 3/4 to full speed.

Participation:
The entire team, half at each end.

Variations:
Many options can be used, i.e., pass from opposite corner to swinging shooter; pass behind the net around the boards to shooter who then swings out; alternating forward and backward skating (skate backwards, take pass, turn and skate forward to shoot).

Break off of the Wings 1

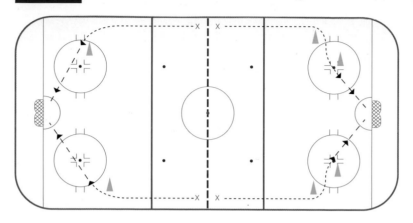

Purpose:

To provide a drill that has the players breaking off of the wings to shoot.

Description:

Performed with players skating down the boards and shooting as they come off of the boards. Obstacles can be placed to set the pattern for the shooters. Practice the different shots and vary the distances.

Tempo:

Drill is executed from 3/4 to full speed.

Participation:

The entire team, half at each end. Drill starts near the red line on the boards.

Variations:

Players can take passes to start drill; change the patterns by moving the obstacles.

Break off of the Wings 2

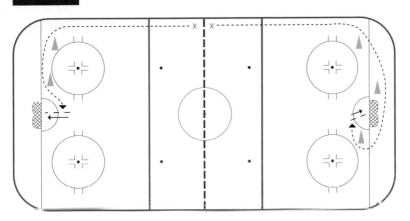

Purpose:
To provide a drill that has the players breaking off of the wings to shoot.

Description:
Performed with players skating down the boards and carrying the puck deep. Obstacles are placed to set patterns that will guide the shooter to the net. The patterns can vary.

Tempo:
Drill is executed from 3/4 to full speed.

Participation:
The entire team, half at each end. Drill starts near the red line on the boards.

Variations:
Players can take passes to start drill; change the patterns by moving the obstacles.

Break off of the Wings 3

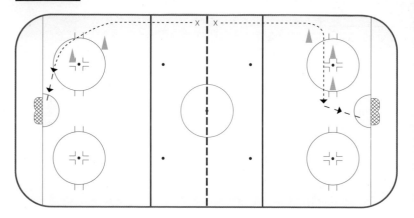

Purpose:
To provide a drill that has the players breaking off of the wings to shoot.

Description:
Performed with players skating down the boards and shooting as they come off of the boards. Obstacles can be placed to set the pattern for the shooter. Both forehand and backhand shots should be practiced.

Tempo:
Drill is executed from 3/4 to full speed.

Participation:
The entire team, half at each end. Drill starts near the red line on the boards.

Variations:
Players can take passes to start drill; change the patterns by moving the obstacles.

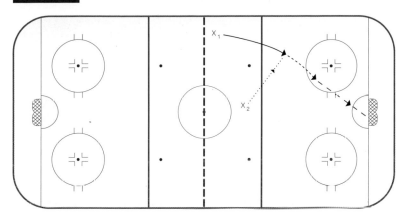

Purpose:

To provide a drill to combine passing and shooting.

Description:

Performed with a player (X_1) breaking off of the boards and taking a shot on net after receiving a pass from a second player (X_2).

Tempo:

Drill is executed from 3/4 to full speed.

Participation:

The entire team, half at each end. Drill starts near the red line on the boards.

Variations:

Player passing the puck moves around to change the spot from where the pass originates.

Pass and Shoot 2

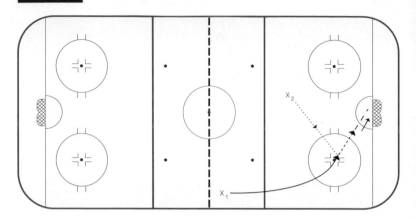

Purpose:

To provide a drill to combine passing and shooting.

Description:

Performed with a player (X_1) breaking to the net from the blue line and taking a shot on net after receiving a pass from a second player (X_2) who is in the middle of the ice.

Tempo:

Drill is executed from 3/4 to full speed.

Participation:

The entire team, half at each end. Drill starts near the red line on the boards.

Variations:

Player passing the puck moves around to change the spot from where the pass originates.

DRILL
83 Pass and Shoot 3

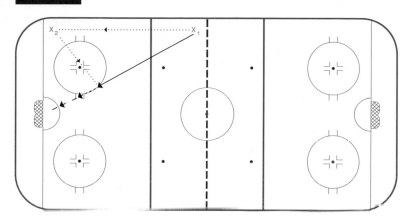

Purpose:
To provide a drill to combine passing and shooting.

Description:
Performed with a player (X_1) breaking off of the boards and taking a shot on net after receiving a pass from a second player (X_2). X_1 initiates drill by passing to X_2 and breaking to the net for a return pass.

Tempo:
Drill is executed from 3/4 to full speed.

Participation:
The entire team, half at each end. Drill starts near the red line on the boards.

Variations:
Player passing the puck moves around to change the spot from where the pass originates.

DRILL
84 Pass and Shoot 4

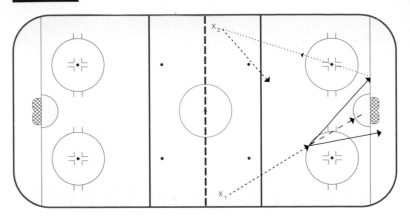

Purpose:

To provide a drill to combine passing and shooting.

Description:

Performed with players on both sides of the ice at the red line. The first player (X_1) skates in and shoots. The player then picks up the rebound (if the player scores, there are loose pucks in the corner) and passes to the second player (X_2). The second player does the same.

Tempo:

Drill is executed at full speed.

Participation:

The entire team, half at each end.

Pass and Shoot 5

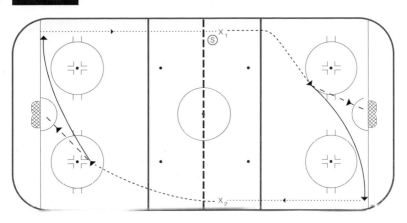

Purpose:

To provide a drill to combine passing and shooting.

Description:

Drill utilizes the whole ice surface with team divided into two groups. The groups are opposite each other at the red line. Loose pucks are in the corners opposite to the players. The first player (X_1) carries the puck and shoots. The player proceeds to the corner, picks up a loose puck and passes to a player in the other group (X_2). The second player (X_2) does the same.

Tempo:

Drill is executed at full speed.

Participation:

The entire team.

Variations:

Players can be placed at different spots to be involved in the passing but not the shooting.

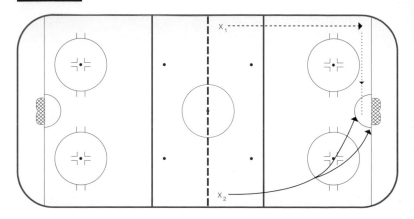

Purpose:

To provide a drill to combine passing and shooting.

Description:

Performed with players on both sides of the ice at the red line. The first player (X_1) carries the puck deep into the end. The second player (X_2) skates toward the net. X_1 passes the puck to X_2 as the player is breaking to the net for the shot.

Tempo:

Drill is executed at full speed.

Participation:

The entire team, half at each end.

Variations:

Obstacles can be added to make the drill more difficult.

Pass and Shoot 7

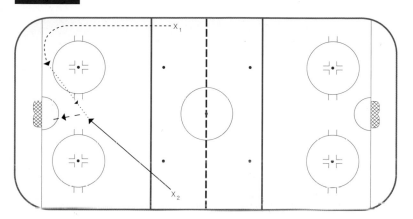

Purpose:

To provide a drill to combine passing and shooting.

Description:

Performed with players on both sides of the ice. The first player (X_1) carries the puck deep into the corner. The second player (X_2) skates into the slot area. X_1 passes the puck to X_2 who is breaking into the slot for the shot.

Tempo:

Drill is executed at full speed.

Participation:

The entire team, half at each end.

Variations:

Obstacles can be added to make the drill more difficult.

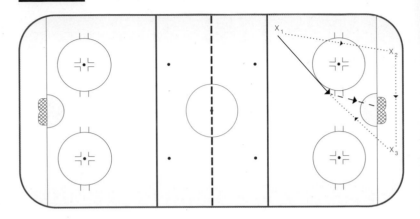

Purpose:

To provide a drill with passing, shooting and player movement.

Description:

Performed with three players. X_1 passes to X_2 and moves into the slot. X_2 passes to X_3, who passes to X_1 in the slot for the shot. X_1 moves to X_3's spot, X3 to X_2's and X_2 to X_1's.

Tempo:

Drill is executed at full speed.

Participation:

The entire team, half at each end.

Variations:

The three players can change where they are located on the ice.

Pass and Shoot 9

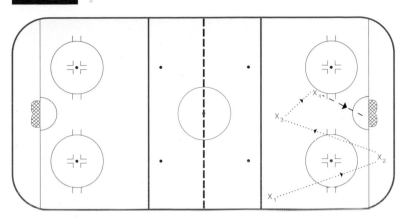

Purpose:

To provide a drill with passing, shooting and player movement.

Description:

Performed with four players. X_1 passes to X_2, X_2 passes to X_3, X_3 passes to X_4 in the slot for the shot. X_1 moves to X_2's spot, X_2 to X_3's, X_3 to X_4's and X_4 to X_1's.

Tempo:

Drill is executed at full speed.

Participation:

The entire team, half at each end.

Variations:

The four players can change where they are located on the ice.

Pass and Shoot 10

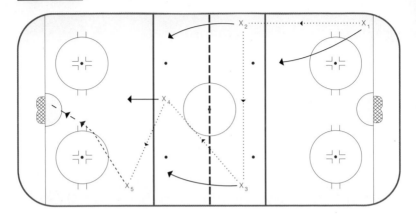

Purpose:

To provide a drill with passing, shooting and player movement.

Description:

Performed with five players. X_1 passes to X_2, X_2 passes to X_3, X_3 passes to X_4, and X_4 passes to X_5. Each player moves into the play so that when X_5 gets the puck there are five players moving toward the net as a unit. X_5 can choose to shoot or pass.

Tempo:

Drill is executed at full speed.

Participation:

The entire team. Team is divided into five-player units.

Variations:

Obstacles can be inserted to make drill more difficult.

Pass and Shoot 11

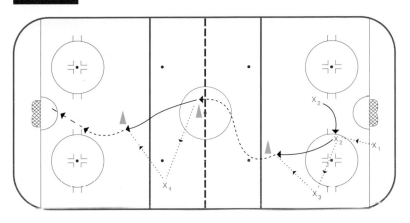

Purpose:

To provide a drill with passing, shooting and player movement.

Description:

Performed with four players. X_1 passes to X_2, X_2 passes to X_3 and moves up the ice for return pass. X_2 passes to X_4 and continues to move up the ice for return pass and a shot opportunity. X_1 moves to X_2's spot, X_2 to X_4's, X_3 to X_1's, and X_4 to X_3's.

Tempo:

Drill is executed at full speed.

Participation:

The entire team.

Variations:

Change the patterns with obstacles.

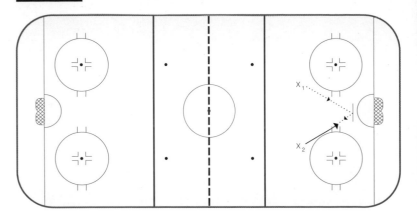

Purpose:
To provide a drill to practice getting rebounds.

Description:
A bench is laid across the goalmouth. One player (X_1) shoots the puck against the bench. The second player (X_2) breaks for the net, goes for the rebound and must shoot over the bench.

Tempo:
Drill is executed at full speed.

Participation:
The entire team, half at each end.

Backhand Shots

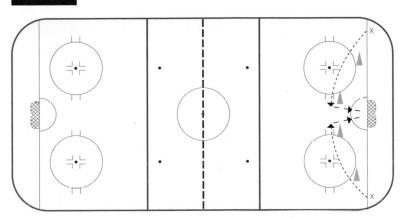

Purpose:

To provide a drill to practice backhand shots.

Description:

Performed with players skating out of the corners to the net. Obstacles can be placed to set patterns.

Tempo:

Drill is executed at full speed.

Participation:

The entire team. Place left hand shooters in one corner and right hand shooters in the other so that when the players approach the net they are naturally on their backhand.

Tip-ins 1

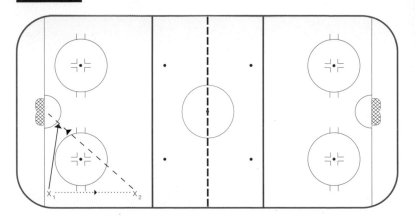

Purpose:

To provide a drill to practice tip-in shots.

Description:

Performed with a player (X_1) in the corner and a player (X_2) on the blue line. X_1 begins the drill by passing to X_2. X_1 moves to the front of the net into position to tip in the shot from X_2.

Tempo:

Drill is executed at full speed.

Participation:

The entire team. Drill can be worked out of four (4) corners.

Variations:

Obstacles can be inserted to force X_1 to work to gain position.

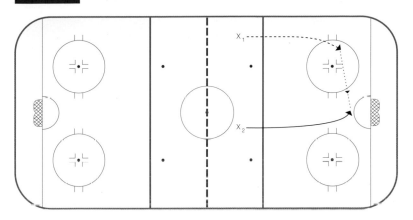

Purpose:
To provide a drill to practice tip-in shots.

Description:
Performed with two players. The first player (X_1) carries the puck deep along the boards. The second player (X_2) breaks for the net. X_1 passes the puck across the goalmouth and X_2 deflects or tips in the puck.

Tempo:
Drill is executed at full speed.

Participation:
The entire team, half at each end.

Variations:
Obstacles can be inserted in the slot area to make it more difficult to complete the pass/shot.

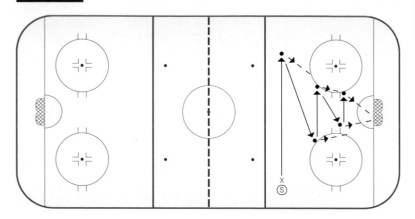

Purpose:

To provide a drill for players to take a number of shots from different spots on the ice.

Description:

Pucks are placed in a pattern that has the shooter skate back and forth. Each puck is closer to the net. The shooter skates to each puck and shoots. The player takes both forehand and backhand shots. Use 4–10 pucks.

Tempo:

Drill is executed at full speed.

Participation:

The entire team, half at each end.

Variations:

Change the pattern of the pucks.

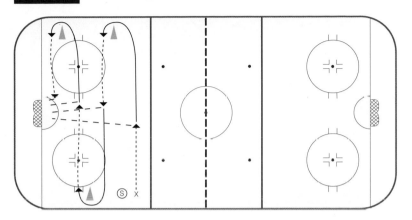

Purpose:

To provide a drill for players to take a number of shots from different spots on the ice.

Description:

Pucks are placed along the boards with each one deeper in the zone. The player picks up the first puck, skates to the middle, shoots, continues to the other side, picks up a puck, skates to the middle and shoots. Continue the drill in this pattern. Obstacles are placed near the boards for the shooter to swing around. Use 4–10 pucks.

Tempo:

Drill is executed at full speed.

Participation:

The entire team, half at each end.

Variations:

Change the location of the obstacles.

Multiple Shots 3

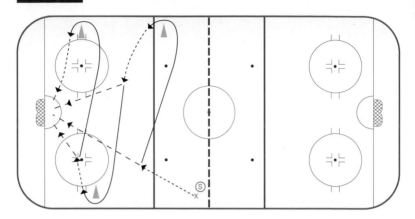

Purpose:

To provide a drill for players to take a number of shots from different spots on the ice.

Description:

Pucks are placed along the boards and one puck is placed just inside the blueline below the face-off dot. The player picks up the first puck, skates toward the net and shoots, continues to the far side, picks up a puck, skates toward the net and shoots. Obstacles are placed for the shooter to swing around. Use 4–10 pucks.

Tempo:

Drill is executed at full speed.

Participation:

The entire team, half at each end.

Variations:

Change the location of the obstacles.

Multiple Shots 4

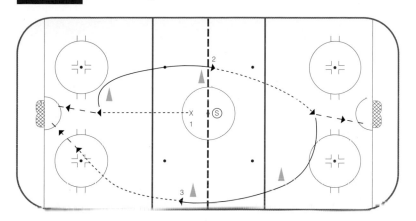

Purpose:

To provide a drill for players to take a number of shots from different spots on the ice.

Description:

Pucks are placed in three spots in the neutral zone. The player starts at one spot, skates in and shoots. The player then swings back to the neutral zone, picks up a second puck, skates in and shoots. Repeat the process for the third puck. Obstacles are placed for the shooter to swing around.

Tempo:

Drill is executed at full speed.

Participation:

The entire team, one player at a time. This is a good competitive game-type drill. Players keep track of goals. Play until there is a winner.

Variations:

Change the location of the pucks.

First to Score

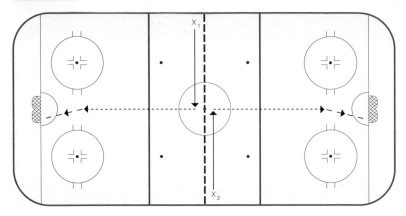

Purpose:

To provide a competitive shooting drill.

Description:

Performed with two players. Players line up on the red line on opposite boards. On the whistle, they skate to center ice and each pick up a puck. The first to score is the winner. Normally, the winners continue to play against other winners until there is a final winner.

Tempo:

Drill is executed at full speed.

Participation:

The entire team.

CHAPTER 5

Conditioning

"... it took me quite a while as a coach to realize that the great majority of players would not pay the price of conditioning unless they were driven."

John Wooden
They Call Me Coach

*Most drills in this chapter suggest the use of intervals to adequately rest players. The intervals are expressed in work to rest ratios: an interval recommendation of 1:3 is one work interval for every three rest intervals.

Intervals 1

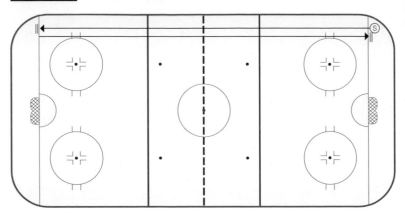

Purpose:

To provide a drill for anaerobic conditioning.

Description:

Performed by skating from goal line to goal line and back again.

Participation:

Team is divided into three to five groups.

Intervals:

1:3 to 1:5; 8 to 12 repetitions at 80% to 85% intensity.

Intervals 2

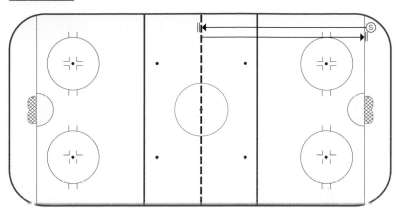

Purpose:
To provide a drill for anaerobic conditioning

Description:
Performed by skating from goal line to red line and back again.

Participation:
Team is divided into three to five groups.

Intervals:
1:3 to 1:5; 8 to 12 repetitions at 90% to 100% intensity.

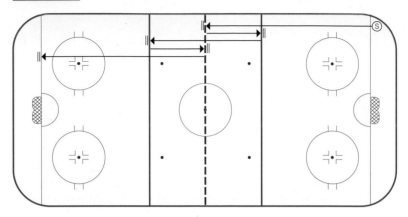

Purpose:
To provide a drill for anaerobic conditioning.

Description:
Performed by skating from goal line to goal line with intervals between the red and blue lines.

Participation:
Team is divided into three to five groups.

Intervals:
1:3 to 1:5; 8 to 12 repetitions at 80% to 85% intensity.

Intervals 4

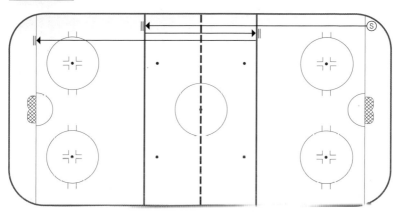

Purpose:

To provide a drill for anaerobic conditioning.

Description:

Performed by skating from goal line to goal line with intervals between the blue lines.

Participation:

Team is divided into three to five groups.

Intervals:

1:3 to 1:5; 8 to 12 repetitions at 80% to 85% intensity.

Intervals 5

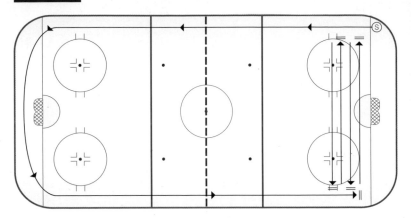

Purpose:
To provide a drill for anaerobic conditioning.

Description:
Performed by skating a lap (from goal line, around the opposite goal, and back to the goal line), then back and forth across the ice twice.

Participation:
Team is divided into four to six groups. There should be only three to five players in each group.

Intervals:
1:4 to 1:6; 6 to 8 repetitions at 70% to 80% intensity.

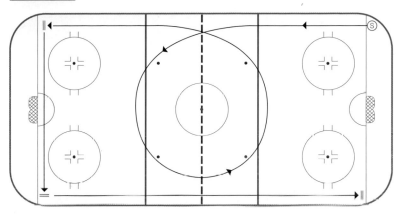

Purpose:

To provide a drill for anaerobic conditioning.

Description:

Performed by making a big loop in the neutral zone while skating from goal line to goal line. Players then skate across the goal line to the far boards, and then along the boards to the far goal line.

Participation:

Team is divided into four to six groups. There should be only three to five players in each group.

Intervals:

1:4 to 1:6; 6 to 8 repetitions at 70% to 80% intensity.

Intervals 7

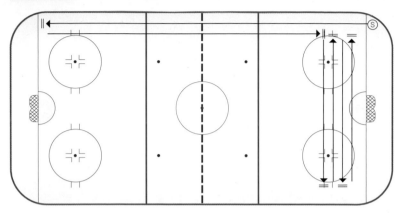

Purpose:

To provide a drill for anaerobic conditioning.

Description:

Performed by skating the length of the ice and back, then back and forth across the ice twice.

Participation:

Team is divided into four to six groups. There should only be three to five players in each group.

Intervals:

1:4 to 1:6; 6 to 8 repetitions at 70% to 80% intensity.

Intervals 8

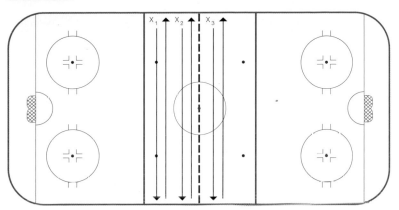

Purpose:
To provide a drill for anaerobic conditioning.

Description:
Players skate across the ice, stop, and come back.
Performed in groups of three, the first player goes,
followed by the second and then the third.

Participation:
The entire team; team is divided into groups of three.

Intervals:
1:2; 8 to 12 repetitions at 80% to 90% intensity.

Intervals 9

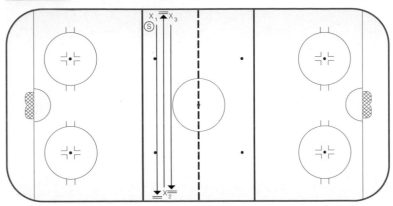

Purpose:

To provide a drill for anaerobic conditioning.

Description:

A relay drill performed in groups of three. The first player (X_1) skates to the far boards and stops. The second player (X_2) does the same. Continue the drill in this fashion.

Participation:

The entire team.

Intervals:

1:2; 8 to 12 repetitions at 100% intensity.

Retrieve Pucks

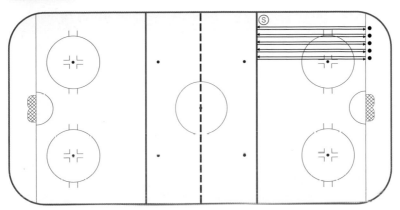

Purpose:

To provide a drill for anaerobic conditioning.

Description:

Pucks (3–5) are lined up on the blue line. A player skates from the goal line to the blue line, stops, picks up a puck, skates back to goal line, stops, drops the puck, continues on for the other pucks.

Participation:

The entire team. Players can work in groups of two or four. First player brings pucks back to the goal line, second player takes pucks to the blue line, and so forth.

Intervals:

1:4; 80% to 90% intensity.

DRILL 111 **Time Intervals 1**

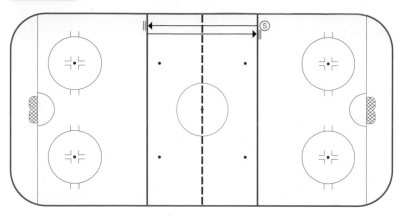

Purpose:

To provide a drill for anaerobic conditioning.

Description:

Performed by skating from blue line to blue line and back again. Drill is executed for a specific time period.

Participation:

Team is divided into two to four groups.

Intervals:

1:3 to 1:4; at 80% to 90% intensity. Time period: 15 to 30 seconds.

Time Intervals 2

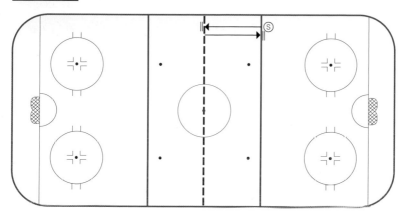

Purpose:

To provide a drill for anaerobic conditioning.

Description:

Performed by skating from blue line to red line and back again. Drill is executed for a specific time period.

Participation:

Team is divided into two to four groups.

Intervals:

1:3 to 1:4; at 80% to 90% intensity. Time period: 15 to 30 seconds.

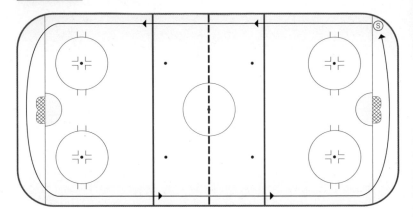

Purpose:
To provide a drill for anaerobic conditioning.

Description:
Performed by skating a full lap.

Participation:
Team is divided into three to five groups.

Intervals:
1:3 to 1:5; 8 to 12 repetitions at 80% to 85% intensity.

Laps 2

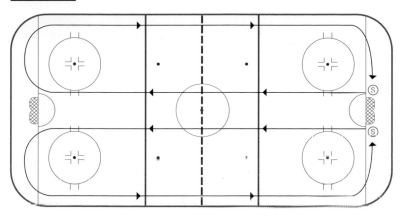

Purpose:

To provide a drill for anaerobic conditioning.

Description:

Performed by skating up the middle, swinging deep into the corners and skating back along the boards.

Participation:

Team is divided into three to five groups.

Intervals:

1:3 to 1:5; 8 to 12 repetitions at 80% to 85% intensity.

Laps 3

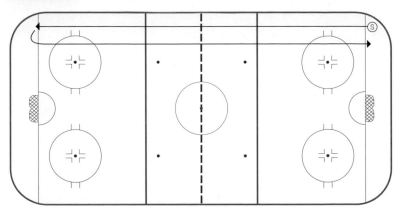

Purpose:

To provide a drill for anaerobic conditioning.

Description:

Players skate the length of the ice, turn, and come back easy.

Participation:

Team is divided into three to five groups.

Intervals:

1:3 to 1:5; 8 to 12 repetitions at 90% to 100% intensity.

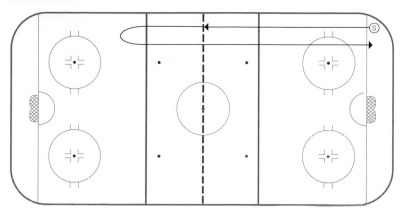

Purpose:

To provide a drill for anaerobic conditioning.

Description:

Performed by skating to the red line and swinging toward the far blue line. Players come back hard from red line to goal line.

Participation:

Team is divided into three to five groups.

Intervals:

1:3 to 1:5; 8 to 12 repetitions at 90% to 100% intensity.

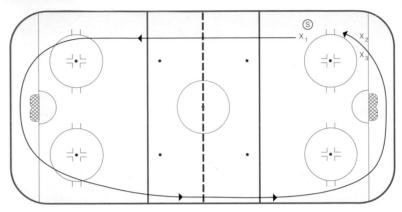

Purpose:

To provide a drill for anaerobic conditioning.

Description:

Performed with one player on top of the face-off circle and two to four on the goal line. The group of players chase X_1. An option is to have a different player take the lead for each lap and to keep times for each group.

Participation:

The entire team.

Intervals:

1:4 to 1:6; 80% to 85% intensity. Time period: 15 to 60 seconds.

"Let's Dance"

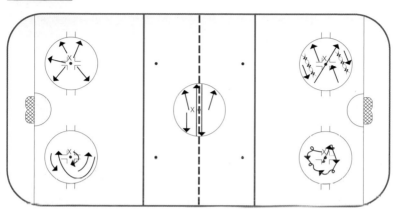

Purpose:

To provide a drill for anaerobic conditioning.

Description:

Performed with one player in each face-off circle.
The players, for a specific time period, make constant
movement. Movement can be any type of activity:
skating, exercises, dance moves, etc.

Participation:

Team is divided into five-player units.

Intervals:

1:3 to 1:4; 4 to 6 repetitions at 90% to 100% intensity.
Time period: 15 to 30 seconds.

2-0/1-1

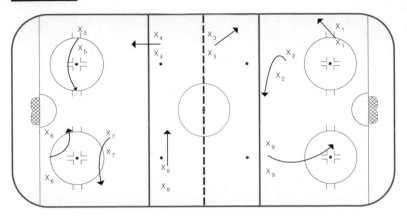

Purpose:

To provide a competitive drill for anaerobic conditioning.

Description:

Performed in pairs. Drill is divided into three segments: 2–0, 1–1, rest. 2–0 segment has players passing the puck back and forth. 1–1 segment has two players fighting for control of the puck. Rest of the segment is light skating.

Participation:

The entire team.

Intervals:

1:1:2 (2–0, 1–1, rest); 4 to 8 repetitions at 85% to 90% intensity. Time intervals: 10 to 15 seconds.

Breakout

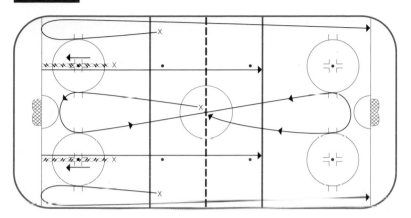

Purpose:

To provide a drill for anaerobic conditioning with the team's breakout system.

Description:

The players execute the positional breakout patterns for coming out of their own end. The players should interchange with the different positions to be familiar with the different patterns.

Participation:

Team is divided into five-player units.

Intervals:

1:3 or 1:4. For short anaerobic bursts at 95% to 100%, each unit would go right after each other. For longer anaerobic training, time periods of 20 to 40 seconds can be used. This means that the units would make multiple rushes and can do it both ways, or go one way, return, and go again.

Aerobic 1

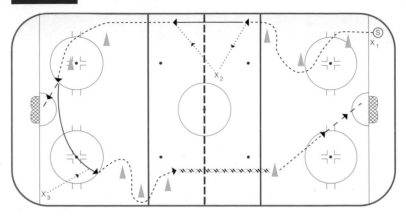

Purpose:

To provide a drill for aerobic conditioning.

Description:

Performed by combining different skill drills while skating a lap. X_1 starts by skating through the obstacles with a puck, then passes to X_2 and receives a return pass and continues on for a shot. X_1 then swings across the ice and receives a pass from X_3, moves up the ice with the puck, turns at the red line and skates backwards to the blue line, turns forward, and goes in for a shot.

Participation:

Team is divided into two groups, one is on the ice, the other rests. Groups execute the drill for a specific time period with continuous activity. Players repeat drill several times during the time period.

Intervals:

60% to 80% intensity. Time period: 5 to 8 minutes.

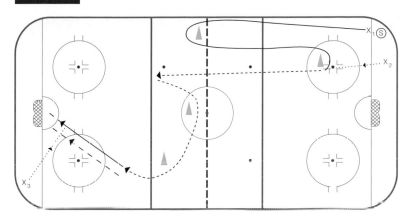

Purpose:

To provide a drill for aerobic conditioning.

Description:

Performed by combining different skill drills while skating a pattern. X_1 starts by skating to the red line. The player swings around the obstacle and heads back toward the goal line. X_1 receives a pass from X_2, and skates up the ice following the pattern laid out with obstacles. X_1 takes a long shot from the blue line, breaks for the net, receives a pass from X_3, and takes a second shot. X_1 then returns to the starting point.

Participation:

Team is divided into two groups, one is on the ice, the other rests. Groups execute the drill for a specific time period with continuous activity. Players repeat drill several times during the time period.

Intervals:

60% to 80% intensity. Time period: 5 to 8 minutes.

Aerobic 3

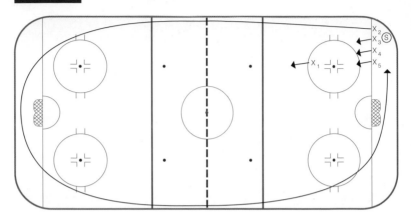

Purpose:
To provide a drill for aerobic conditioning.

Description:
Players skate laps for a specific time period. Each group of players skate as a group and stay together. Each player should take turns leading the group.

Participation:
Team is divided into groups of 4 to 6 players. Two groups execute the drill simultaneously while the others rest.

Intervals:
60% to 80% intensity. Time period: 5 to 8 minutes.

Winner Rests

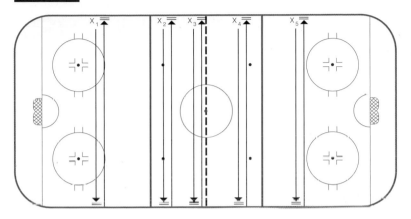

Purpose:

To provide a competitive conditioning drill.

Description:

Performed with players lined up along the boards. Players skate to far boards, stop and return. Winner gets to rest.

Tempo:

Drill is executed at full speed.

Participation:

The entire team.

Variations:

Drill can be executed with laps, or over and back twice, or red line to blue line and back, etc.

1 on 1 Conditioning

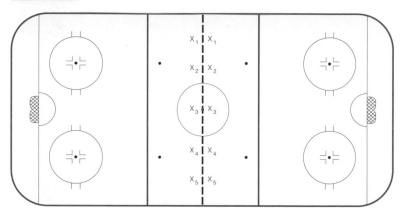

Purpose:

To provide a conditioning drill that is competitive.

Description:

Games of 1 on 1 are played simultaneously. Drill is executed for specific time period.

Participation:

The entire team. Part or all the players can execute the drill. Players can use the entire ice or be limited (i.e., 1 on 1 games in each zone).

Intervals:

90% to 100% intensity. Time period: 30 to 120 seconds.

CHAPTER 6

Goaltending

" But once again, my belief was substantiated that a youngster must practice self-discipline and get his game under control if he is to reach individual stardom and the team success. "

John Wooden
They Call Me Coach

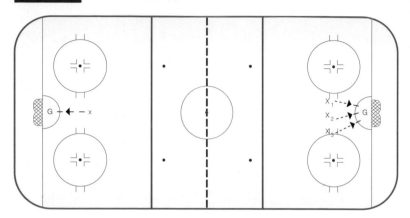

Purpose:

To provide a warm-up drill for goalies.

Description:

Performed with one to three players taking shots at the goalie. Shots are easy, directed at specific spots (i.e., catching glove, blocker, lower left side, etc.). Drill enables goalie to loosen up and get the feel of the puck.

Participation:

Goalie, small number of shooters.

Random Shots 1

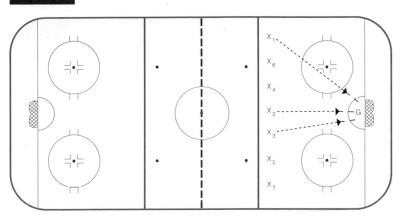

Purpose:

To provide a warm up drill for goalies

Description:

Performed with five to 12 players lined up across the ice in front of the goalie. The distance can vary. Each player has a number, unknown to the goalie. The players shoot in numeric order, no matter where they are placed on the ice. This forces the goalie to react quickly to the person shooting.

Participation:

Goalie, large number of shooters.

Random Shots 2

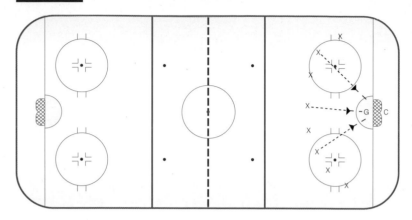

Purpose:

To provide a warm-up drill for goalies.

Description:

Performed with five to 12 players lined up across the ice in front of the goalie. The distance can vary. The coach is behind the net and points to the player that will shoot. This forces the goalie to react quickly to the person shooting. It also means the shooters all must be prepared to shoot since they could be picked next.

Participation:

Goalie, large number of shooters, coach.

Movement 1

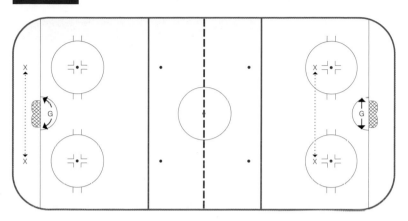

Purpose:

To provide a drill to train the goalie to move in the goal area.

Description:

Performed with two players passing the puck between themselves. The goalie moves with the puck. If the players are in front, the goalie's movements are out high to cut down the angle of the potential shooter. If the players are behind the net, the goalie's movements are deep in the net to protect both goal posts.

Participation:

Goalie, two players.

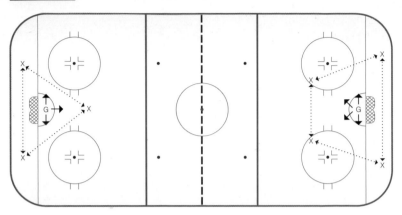

Purpose:

To provide a drill to train the goalie to move in the goal area.

Description:

Performed with three or four players passing the puck. The goalie moves with the puck. The three players are in a triangle shape, and the four players are in a box shape. The goalie has to move both in tight to protect the goal posts and out high to cut down the angle of potential shots.

Participation:

Goalie, three or four players.

Movement 3

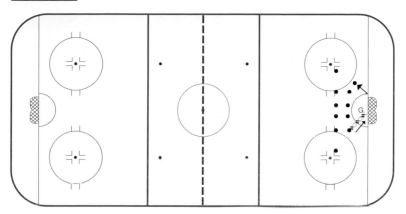

Purpose:

To provide a drill to train the goalie to move out and clear the puck.

Description:

Pucks are lined up 5 to 15 feet from the crease. The goalie moves out and clears the first puck, backs into his crease, moves out to clear the second puck, and so on. Practice clearing the puck both on forehand and backhand. Practice one-handed and two-handed clearing.

Participation:

Goalie.

Movement 4

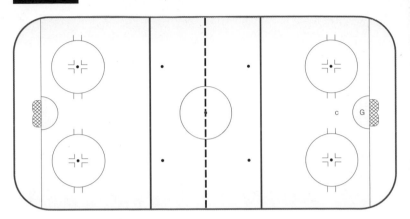

Purpose:

To provide a drill to train the goalie to make quick body movements.

Description:

The coach stands a few feet (7–10) in front of the goalie. The coach points in different directions and the goalie responds with the appropriate movement to make a save. The goalie, after each movement, returns quickly to his goalie stance. For example, the coach points high, the goalie moves to make a glove save. If the coach points low to the side, the goalie moves to make a leg save.

Participation:

Goalie, coach.

Movement 5

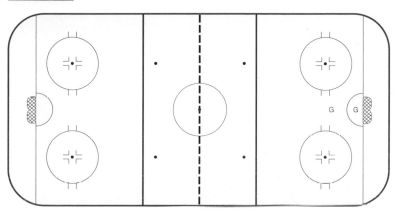

Purpose:
To provide a drill to train the goalie to make quick body movements.

Description:
Two goalies stand five feet apart. One goalie leads, the other follows. The lead goalie will make movements and the second goalie will follow. This "mirror" like drill teaches quick reactions.

Participation:
Two goalies.

134 Movement 6

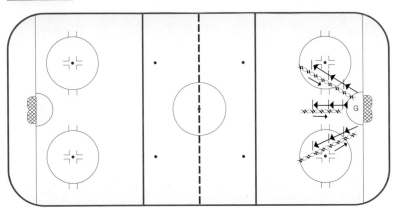

Purpose:

To provide a drill to improve the goalie's agility.

Description:

Hockey sticks are laid down in front of the goal in some order, usually straight lines. The goalie, moving and maintaining his goalie stance, moves out stepping over the sticks. When the goalie reaches the end, the drill is repeated going backwards.

Participation:

Goalie, one shooter.

Variations:

Flip pucks high while the goalie is moving in order for the goalie to make glove saves.

Movement 7

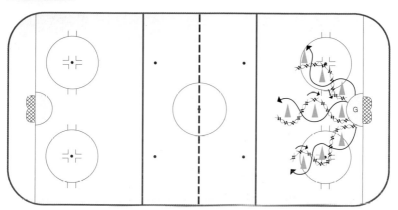

Purpose:

To provide a drill to improve the goalie's agility.

Description:

Obstacles are laid out in front of the goal in some order, usually straight lines. The goalie, moving and maintaining his goalie stance, skates through the obstacles. When the goalie reaches the end, the drill is repeated going backwards.

Participation:

Goalie, one shooter.

Variations:

Have the goalie stickhandle pucks; flip pucks high while the goalie is moving in order for the goalie to make glove saves.

Movement 8

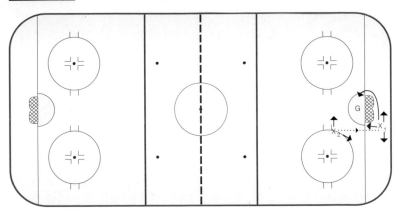

Purpose:
To provide a drill to train the goalie to make quick body movements.

Description:
Two players, one in front and one behind the net, pass the puck back and forth. They are also moving in different directions. The goalie moves with the puck and with the players' movements.

Participation:
Goalie, two players.

Variations:
Give the players the option to shoot.

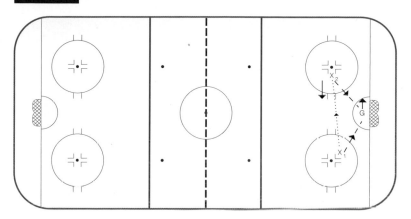

Purpose:

To provide a drill for goalies to stop shots after a pass.

Description:

Two players (X_1 and X_2) line up in front of the goal. X_1 can shoot or pass, X_2 can only shoot. The goalie must move with the pass.

Participation:

Goalie, two players.

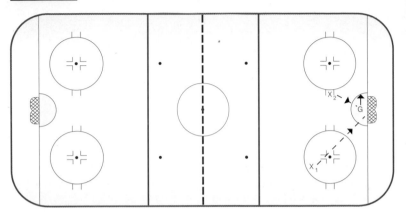

Purpose:

To provide a drill for goalies to stop shots and rebounds.

Description:

Two players are in front of the goal. X_1 is 20 to 35 feet out, X_2 is 5 to 10 feet out. Both players have pucks. X_1 shoots on goal. X_2 quickly shoots after the goalie has stopped X_1's shot. X_2's shot simulates a rebound. The goalie has to move quickly after making the first save.

Participation:

Goalie, two players.

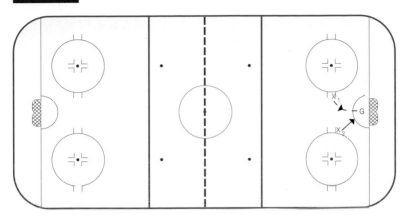

Purpose:

To provide a drill for goalies to stop shots and rebounds.

Description:

Two players are in front of the goal. X_1 shoots and X_2 moves for the rebound. Drill places emphasis on rebounds so X_1's shots are such that rebounds will usually result.

Participation:

Goalie, two players.

DRILL 140 Shots 4

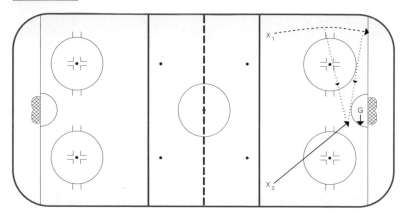

Purpose:

To provide a drill for goalies to practice stopping tip-ins.

Description:

Two players are in front of the goal. X_1 carries the puck, and X_2 moves toward goal in the direction of the far goal post. X_1 has the option of shooting to keep the goalie honest. X_1's purpose is to get the puck to X_2 for an in tight shot or tip-in and force the goalie to react quickly for such a shot.

Participation:

Goalie, two players.

141 Shots 5

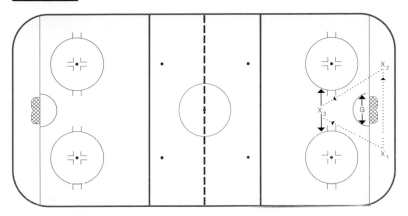

Purpose:

To provide a drill for goalies to stop shots from the slot after a pass from behind the net.

Description:

Three players are in a triangle with X_1 and X_2 behind the net and X_3 in the slot. X_1 and X_2 pass the puck between themselves and to X_3 who shoots. X_3 also moves around in the slot to be in position for a pass from behind the net.

Participation:

Goalie, three players.

142 Shots 6

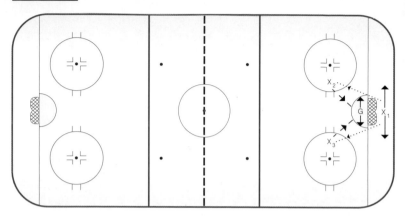

Purpose:

To provide a drill for goalies to stop shots from the slot after a pass from behind the net.

Description:

Three players are in a triangle with X_1 behind the net and X_2 and X_3 in the slot. X_1 moves behind the net and passes the puck to the shooters. The shooters have the option of shooting or passing back to X_1.

Participation:

Goalie, three players.

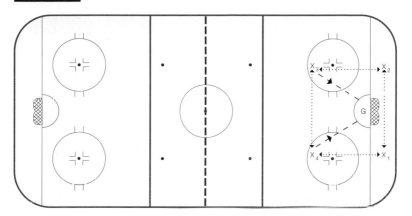

Purpose:

To provide a drill for goalies to stop shots from the slot after a pass from behind the net.

Description:

Four players are in a box with X_1 and X_2 behind the net and X_3 and X_4 in the slot. X_1 and X_2 pass the puck between themselves and to X_3 and X_4. X_3 and X_4 have the options of shooting, passing between themselves, or passing back to X_1 and X_2.

Participation:

Goalie, four players.

Shots 8

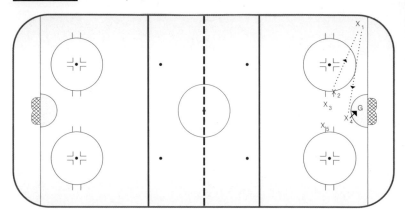

Purpose:

To provide a drill for the goalies to stop shots from the slot after a pass from the corner.

Description:

One player, X_1, is in the corner and the other players are scattered in the slot area. X_1 passes to the other players who shoot.

Participation:

Goalie, four to eight players.

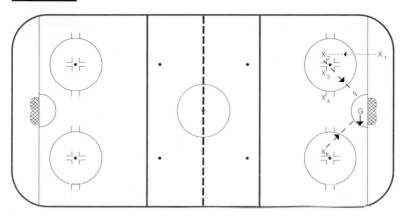

Purpose:

To provide a drill to train the goalie for shots and rebounds in the slot when the other team has puck control deep in the zone.

Description:

Performed with four to eight players. One player, X_1, passes the pucks out from behind the goal line to a group of players. Another player, X_5, is off to the side with some pucks. X_5 shoots quickly after each shot from the other players, forcing the goalie to play the second shots like rebounds.

Participation:

Goalie, four to eight players.

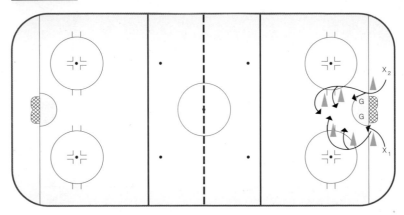

Purpose:

To provide a drill for goalies to stop shots from players coming from deep in the zone or behind the net.

Description:

Obstacles are laid out to set patterns for the player to come from deep toward the goal. The player can either attempt to jam the puck or move for a shot. Drill should have two players, one working from each side.

Participation:

Goalie, two players.

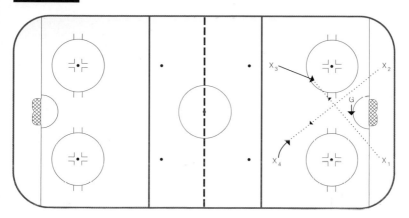

Purpose:

To provide a drill for goalies to stop shots from above the circles on passes through the slot.

Description:

Two players, X_1 and X_2, are behind the goal line and two players, X_3 and X_4, are near the blue line. The players deep are the passers, and the others are the shooters. X_1 passes to X_3, and X_2 passes to X_4. The shooters receive a pass and move toward the net and shoot.

Participation:

Goalie, four players.

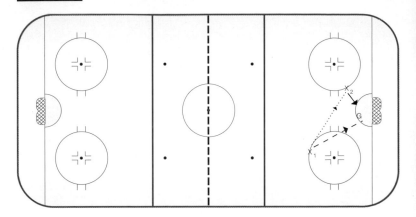

Purpose:

To provide a drill for the goalie to make saves with an offensive player at the edge of the crease.

Description:

Two players are in front of the net, X_1 is out and X_2 is at the edge of the crease. X_1 shoots. X_2 moves to act as a screen for a tip-in, or a rebound.

Participation:

Goalie, two players.

Shots 13

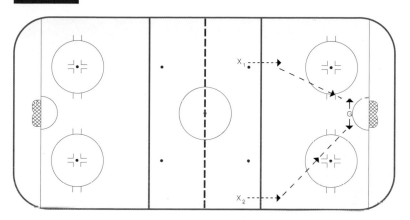

Purpose:

To provide a drill for the goalie to stop wide angle shots.

Description:

Two players are wide, one on each side. They skate in alternately, taking wide shots. Drill forces the goalie to move quickly side to side.

Participation:

Goalie, two players.

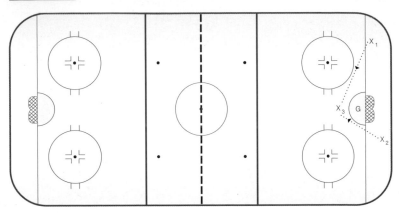

Purpose:

To provide a drill to train the goalie to intercept or deflect passes intended for the player in the slot.

Description:

Three players are involved with two in deep in the zone and one near the crease. The deep players make passes to the player near the crease and the goalie deflects the passes.

Participation:

Goalie, three players.

CHAPTER 7

Checking

"Over the years, I have become convinced that every detail is important and that success usually accompanies attention to little details. It is this, in my judgment, that makes for the difference between champion and near champion."

John Wooden
They Call Me Coach

DRILL
151 Forechecking 1

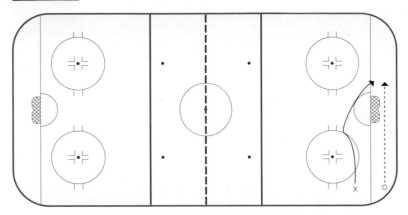

Purpose:

To provide a drill to teach forwards to check the puck carrier.

Description:

An offensive player (O) carries the puck behind the goal line. The checking forward (X) skates parallel to O staying a half-stride behind while maintaining the same speed, thus forcing O to go behind the net. On the far side of the net X moves below the goal line to force O to the boards.

Participation:

Two players. Drill can be executed at both ends.

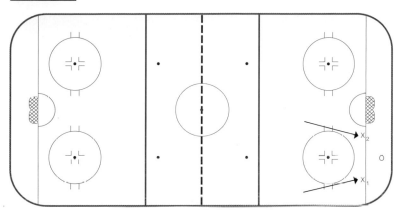

Purpose:

To provide a drill to teach two forwards to pressure the puckcarrier.

Description:

The puck carrier (O) starts a few feet ahead of the first forechecker (X_1). X_1 forces O to the boards in the direction of the net. The second forechecker (X_2) moves in from a different direction. The first forechecker should play the body, and the second takes the puck.

Participation:

Three players. Drill can be executed at both ends.

Forechecking 3

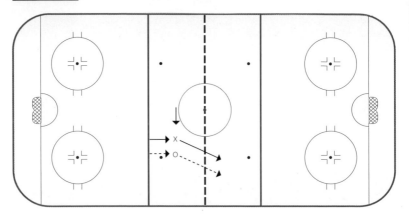

Purpose:

To provide a drill to teach 1 on 1 forechecking in the neutral zone.

Description:

An offensive player (O) skates up the ice with a puck. The forechecker (X) moves to the puck carrier. X's objective is to force O toward the boards and into a passing situation. The forechecker should always play the body after the puck has been passed.

Participation:

Two players. Drill can be executed on both sides in the neutral zone.

Forechecking 4

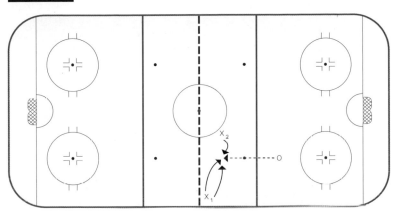

Purpose:

To provide a drill to teach the center and puckside wing to forecheck as a tandem in the neutral zone.

Description:

An offensive player (O) moves up the ice with the puck. The center (X_2) pressures O toward the puckside wing (X_1) who can then double team the puck carrier.

Participation:

Three players.

DRILL 155 — Wings Check in Neutral Zone

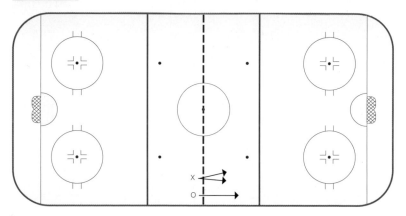

Purpose:

To provide a drill to teach wingers close checking in the neutral zone.

Description:

An offensive forward (O) without the puck skates along the boards in the neutral zone. The defensive forward (X) stays close to O preventing the offensive forward from getting ahead or cutting to the middle. The checker (X), without running interference, is allowed to play the body to prevent O from cutting to the middle.

Participation:

Two players. Drill can be executed on both sides in the neutral zone.

Defense 1

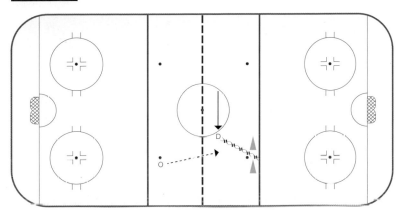

Purpose:

To provide a drill to teach the defense to play offensive players in open ice.

Description:

Two obstacles are placed in the neutral zone to restrict the offensive forward's (O) mobility. O carries the puck up the ice and the defenseman (D) makes a play by the blue line. O, staying within the obstacles, attempts to beat the defenseman or dump the puck. If O dumps the puck, D plays the body.

Participation:

Two players; defenseman and forward.

Defense 2

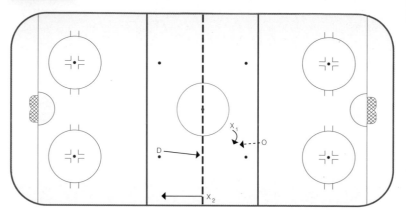

Purpose:

To provide a drill to teach the defense to stand up in the neutral zone.

Description:

This drill is similar to Drill 154 with a defender added. The defenseman (D) stands up at the red line to play the puck carrier (O) who is being pressured by the center (X_1). X_2 backchecks and covers for D.

Participation:

Four players: one offensive player, two defensive forwards, one defenseman.

Defense 3

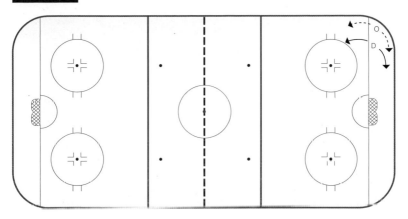

Purpose:

To provide a drill to teach the defense to check the puck carrier in the defensive zone.

Description:

An offensive player (O) attempts to skate out of the corner with the puck. The defenseman (D) plays the body by keeping O to the outside and staying between the puck and the net. D plays O, separating the player from the puck.

Participation:

Two players; forward and defenseman.

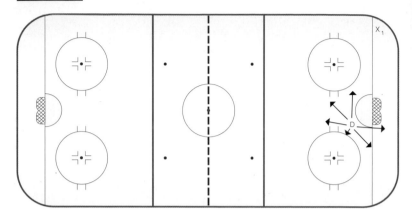

Purpose:

To provide a drill to teach the defense proper positioning in front of the net.

Description:

The defenseman (D) lines up on top of the crease in line with the far goal post facing X_1, who has the puck in the corner. This permits the defensive player to view the entire puckside area while not allowing anyone entrance to the net from the far side. This positioning allows D to move to the opposition or to the puck.

Participation:

Two players; one defenseman.

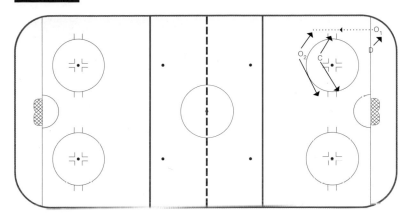

Purpose:

To provide a drill to teach the center to defend the
slot area.

Description:

The center (C) stays with an offensive player (O_2) in the
slot area. A second offensive player (O_1) is in the corner
with a puck. A defender (D) plays O_1. O_1 attempts to pass
to O_2 and the center must keep O_2 in check.

Participation:

Four players; two offensive players, one defense and one
defensive forward.

Wings

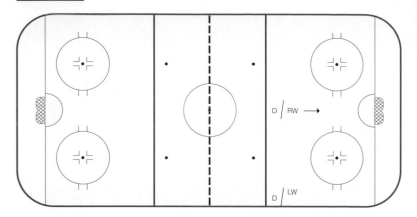

Purpose:

To provide a drill to teach wingers proper position covering the points.

Description:

The drill teaches the puckside wing to cover the point closely and the off-side wing to cover both the high slot and the point. The point players can move around to force the wingers to adjust. Also, a player in the corner can attempt to pass to the point with the wings adjusting.

Participation:

Four players; two offensive defenders and two defensive wingers. Option of inserting an offensive forward with the puck.

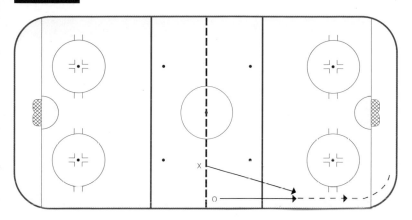

Purpose:

To provide a drill to teach forwards to play the man.

Description:

An offensive player (O) skates along the boards and dumps the puck in. A defensive forward (X) takes O into the boards, either before or after O dumps the puck in.

Participation:

Two forwards.

Play the Man 2

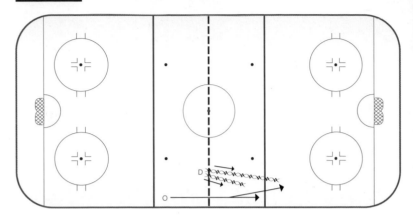

Purpose:

To provide a drill to teach the defense to play the offensive forward after the puck is dumped in.

Description:

An offensive forward (O) skates along the boards and dumps the puck in. A defenseman (D), skating backwards, plays O and takes the player into the boards.

Participation:

Two players; an offensive forward and a defenseman.

Play the Man 3

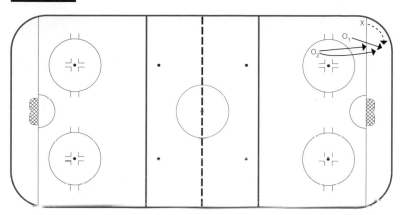

Purpose:

To provide a drill to teach offensive forwards to play the man in the offensive zone.

Description:

A defensive player (X), who can be either a forward or a defenseman, has the puck. Two offensive forwards O_1 and O_2 converge on X. O_1 plays the man and O_2 takes the puck.

Participation:

Three players; a defensive player and two offensive players.

Play the Man 4

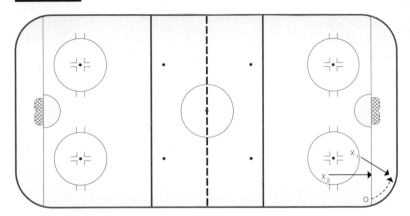

Purpose:

To provide a drill to teach the defensive players to play the man when the offensive player is deep in the zone.

Description:

An offensive player (O) has the puck deep in the offensive zone and is carrying the puck. The first defensive player (X_1) normally, but not always, a defenseman, plays the body; and the second defensive player (X_2) takes the puck.

Participation:

Three players; an offensive player and two defensive players.

DRILL

166 Play the Man 5

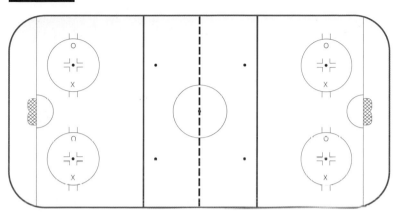

Purpose:

To provide a drill to teach playing the man in open space.

Description:

Two players, an offensive (O) and a defensive (X) player are inside the face-off circle. Within the confines of the circle, O tries to get by X. Sticks and puck are optional. Drill can also be executed with two defensive players and one offensive player.

Participation:

Two or three players, an offensive player and one or two defensive players.

Play the Man 6

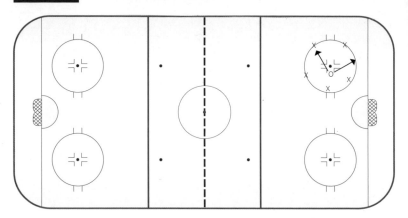

Purpose:

To provide a drill to teach playing the man in open space.

Description:

An offensive player (O) is in the middle of a face-off circle, and a number of defensive players (X) are on the face-off circle edge. O tries to beat the X's and get outside the circle. Sticks and puck are optional.

Participation:

One offensive player and four to six defensive players to each circle.

Play the Man 7

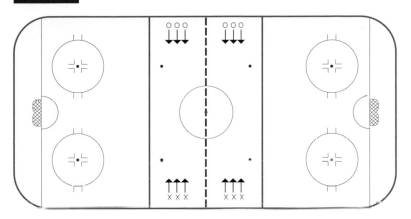

Purpose:
To provide a drill to teach playing the man in open spaces.

Description:
Performed with two groups of players: offensive (O) players with pucks and defensive (X) players without sticks. Each group lines up on opposite boards and skate towards each other. The O's try to beat the X's and the X's attempt to bodycheck the O's.

Participation:
The entire team, two groups.

Play the Man 8

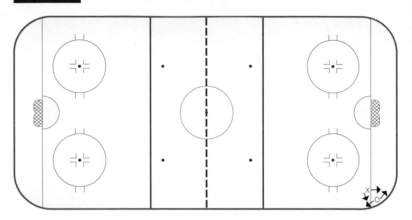

Purpose:

To provide a drill to teach the defensive player to freeze the puck in the defensive zone.

Description:

Two players fight for the puck along the boards. The offensive player (O) attempts to free the puck and the defensive player (X) attempts to freeze the puck and control O.

Participation:

One defensive player and one offensive player.

Play the Man 9

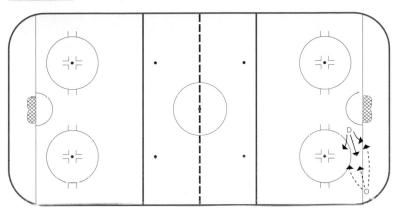

Purpose:

To provide a drill to teach the defense to play the man coming from the corner toward the net.

Description:

An offensive player (O) with a puck comes from the corner or deep in the zone toward the net. The defenseman (D) picks up O and prevents the player from getting to the net area.

Participation:

One offensive player and one defenseman.

Play the Man 10

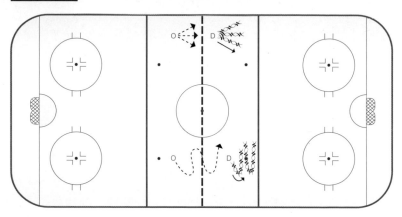

Purpose:

To provide a drill to teach the defense to play the man in the neutral zone.

Description:

An offensive player (O) skates through the neutral zone with the puck. The player may go in any direction or skate in a tight weave pattern. The defenseman (D) skates backwards, prevents O from getting by, and, if possible, attempts to bodycheck O off the puck.

Participation:

Two players, one offensive player and one defenseman.

Play the Man 11

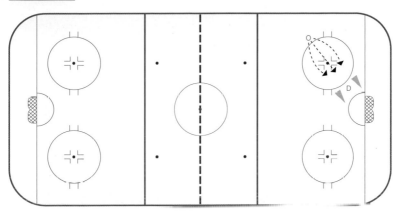

Purpose:

To provide a drill to teach the defensemen to play the man close to the net and to prevent a shot on goal.

Description:

Two obstacles are laid out. The defenseman (D) starts between the two obstacles. The offensive player (O) must skate between the obstacles and deke D and get a shot off. D must play O and prevent him from shooting.

Participation:

Two players, one offensive player and one defenseman.

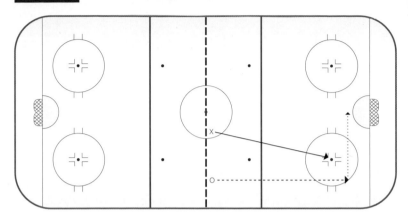

Purpose:

To provide a drill to teach the defensive player to make a "last ditch" save against a pass.

Description:

An offensive player (O) carries the puck down the ice close to the boards. A defensive player (X), coming from behind, dives to block a pass from O. A second offensive player can be inserted to receive the attempted pass.

Participation:

One defensive player and one or two offensive players.

Variations:

For defensive forwards, have players start like a late backchecker and try to get back into the play. For defensemen, have players start by skating backwards, then turning forward, before diving to block the pass.

Blocking Shots

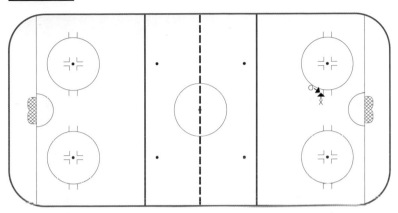

Purpose:

To provide a drill to teach the defensemen to block shots.

Description:

Using tennis balls, an offensive player (O) takes shots. The defensive player (X) blocks the shots. Practice the different blocks: dropping to both knees, sliding with the body, standing erect with feet together and the toes of both skates pointing directly at the shooter.

Participation:

Two players, an offensive player and a defensive player.

Bumping

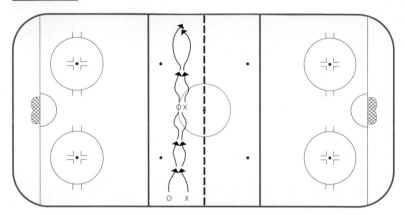

Purpose:

To provide a drill to teach constant contact and strength for contact.

Description:

Performed with players in pairs. Start with no pucks and no sticks, progress to the O's with sticks and pucks and X's with no sticks, and then X's with sticks. Players simply bump each other at close quarters.

Participation:

The entire team divided into pairs.

CHAPTER 8

Situations

" Today's hockey player should be fully aware that it is not the man in possession but the players moving into the open spaces that give any combined movement its impetus. *"*

Horst Wein
The Science of Hockey

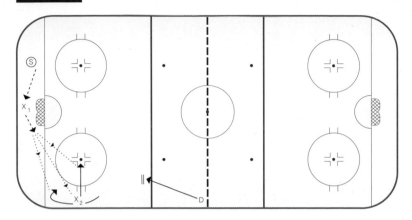

Purpose:
To provide a drill for 1–1 and 2–1's with a breakout pass.

Description:
X_1 makes a breakout pass to X_2 who is on the boards. X_2 turns, in any of a variety of directions, and heads up ice. The defenseman (D) moves up from the red line to play X_2 on the 1–1. To make the drill a 2–1, insert a second forward.

Tempo:
Drill is executed at full speed.

Participation:
Two offensive players and one defenseman. Drill can be worked from both ends alternately.

Variations:
Another offensive player can be added to allow for a second pass to be made prior to the breakout.

1-1/2-1 #2

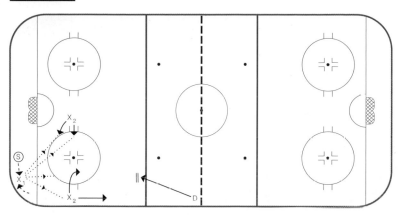

Purpose:

To provide a drill for 1-1 and 2-1's with a breakout pass.

Description:

X_1 makes a breakout pass to X_2 who is in the middle. X_2 can choose to go up ice in a number of directions. The defenseman (D) moves up from the red line to play X_2 on the 1-1. To make the drill a 2-1, insert a second forward.

Tempo:

Drill is executed at full speed.

Participation:

Two offensive players and one defenseman. Drill can be worked from both ends alternately.

Variations:

Another offensive player can be added to allow for a second pass to be made prior to the breakout.

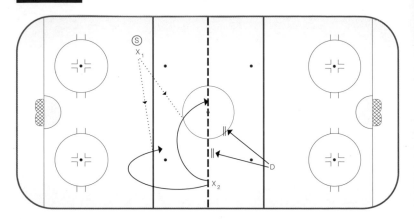

Purpose:

To provide a drill for 1–1 and 2–1's with an outlet pass in the neutral zone.

Description:

X_1, from the blue line area, makes an outlet pass to X_2 who is coming off the boards. The defenseman (D) moves up from inside the blue line to play X_2 on the 1–1. To make the drill a 2–1, insert a second forward.

Tempo:

Drill is executed at full speed.

Participation:

Two offensive players and one defenseman. Drill can be worked in both directions.

Variations:

Another offensive player can be added to allow for a second pass to be made prior to the breakout.

1-1/2-1 #4

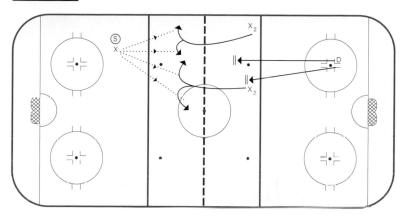

Purpose:

To provide a drill for 1-1 and 2-1's with an outlet pass in the neutral zone.

Description:

X_1, from the blue line area, makes an outlet pass to X_2 who is coming back up the middle or off of the boards close to X_1. The defenseman (D) moves up from inside the blue line to play X_2 on the 1-1. To make the drill a 2-1, insert a second forward.

Tempo:

Drill is executed at full speed.

Participation:

Two offensive players and one defenseman. Drill can be worked in both directions.

Variations:

Another offensive player can be added to allow for a second pass to be made prior to the breakout.

1-1/2-1 #5

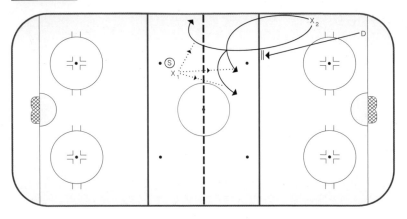

Purpose:

To provide a drill for 1–1 and 2–1's with an outlet pass in the neutral zone.

Description:

X_1, from the red line area, makes an outlet pass to X_2 who is just coming over the blue line. The defenseman (D) moves up from deep in the zone to play X_2 on the 1–1. To make the drill a 2–1, insert a second forward.

Tempo:

Drill is executed at full speed.

Participation:

Two offensive players and one defenseman. Drill can be worked in both directions.

Variations:

Another offensive player can be added to allow for a second pass to be made prior to the breakout.

3-2/3-1 #1

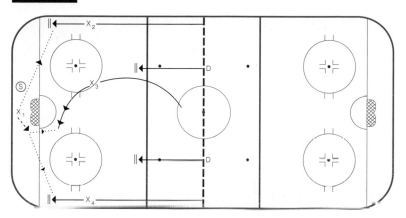

Purpose:

To provide a drill for 3-2 and 3-1's with a breakout pass.

Description:

X_1 makes a breakout pass to X_2, X_3, or X_4. The defense (D) move up from the red line to play the 3-2. To make the drill 3-1, use only one defenseman.

Tempo:

Drill is executed at full speed.

Participation:

Four offensive players and two defensemen for 3-2; one defenseman for 3-1. Drill can be worked in both directions.

Variations:

Another offensive player can be added to allow for a second pass to be made prior to the breakout. Insert a defensive forward for a 3-3 drill.

3-2/3-1 #2

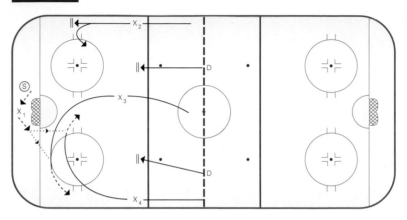

Purpose:

To provide a drill for 3–2 and 3–1's with a breakout pass.

Description:

X_1 makes a breakout pass to either X_3 or X_4 who crisscross in their own end. The defense (D) move up from the red line to play the 3–2. To make the drill 3–1, use only one defenseman.

Tempo:

Drill is executed at full speed.

Participation:

Four offensive players and two defensemen for 3–2; one defenseman for 3–1. Drill can be worked both ways.

Variations:

Another offensive player can be added to allow for a second pass to be made prior to the breakout. Insert a defensive forward for a 3–3 drill.

DRILL
183   3-2/3-1 #3

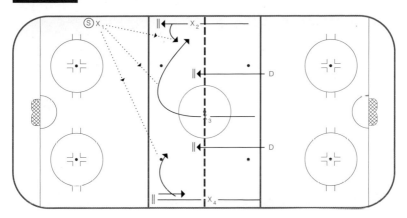

Purpose:

To provide a drill for 3-2 and 3-1's with an outlet pass in the neutral zone.

Description:

X1, from the blue line area, makes an outlet pass to X_2, X_3 or X_4 in the neutral zone. The defense (D) move up from inside the blue line to play the 3-2. To make the drill 3-1, use only one defenseman.

Tempo:

Drill is executed at full speed.

Participation:

Four offensive players and two defensemen for 3-2; one defenseman for 3-1. Drill can be worked in both directions.

Variations:

Another offensive player can be added to allow for a second pass to be made prior to the breakout. Insert a defensive forward for a 3-3 drill.

184 3-2/3-1 #4

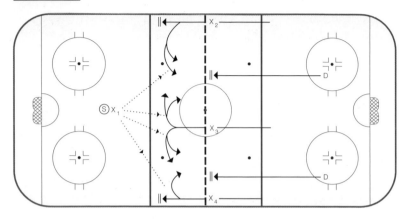

Purpose:

To provide a drill for 3-2 and 3-1's with an outlet pass in the neutral zone.

Description:

X_1, from the blue line area, makes an outlet pass to X_2, X_3 or X_4 in the neutral zone. The defense (D) move up from inside the blue line to play the 3-2. To make the drill 3-1, use only one defenseman.

Tempo:

Drill is executed at full speed.

Participation:

Four offensive players and two defensemen for 3-2; one defenseman for 3-1. Drill can be worked in both directions.

Variations:

Another offensive player can be added to allow for a second pass to be made prior to the breakout. Insert a defensive forward for a 3-3 drill.

3–2/3–1 #5

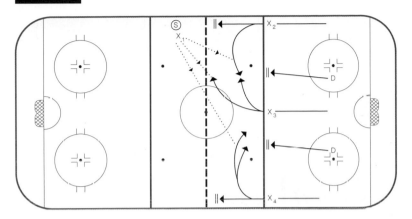

Purpose:
To provide a drill for 3–2 and 3–1's with an outlet pass in the neutral zone.

Description:
X_1, from the red line area, makes an outlet pass to X_2, X_3 or X_4 who are coming out over the blue line. The defense (D) move up from deep in the zone to play the 3–2. To make the drill 3–1, use only one defenseman.

Tempo:
Drill is executed at full speed.

Participation:
Four offensive players and two defensemen for 3–2; one defenseman for 3–1. Drill can be worked in both directions.

Variations:
Another offensive player can be added to allow for a second pass to be made prior to the breakout. Insert a defensive forward for 3–3 drill.

186 Fastbreak 1

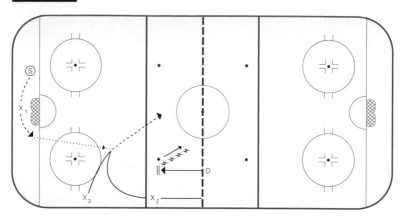

Purpose:

To provide a drill for a fastbreak from the defensive zone.

Description:

X_1, from deep in the zone, makes a pass up the middle to X_2 who is breaking up the middle. The defenseman (D) moves in from the red line to play the 1–1.

Tempo:

Drill is executed at full speed.

Participation:

Two offensive players and one defenseman.

Variations:

Additional offensive players can be inserted to make a multiple-player breakout.

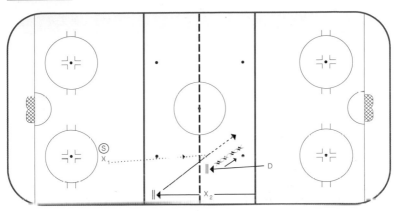

Purpose:
To provide a drill for a fastbreak from the neutral zone.

Description:
X_1, from near in the blue line, passes up the middle to X_2 who is cutting through the middle. The defenseman (D) moves up from his zone to play the 1–1.

Tempo:
Drill is executed at full speed.

Participation:
Two offensive players and one defenseman.

Variations:
Additional offensive players can be inserted to make a multiple-player breakout.

Continuous 3-2

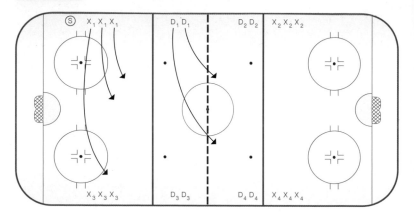

Purpose:

To provide a drill for 3-2 with constant movement.

Description:

Forwards are divided into groups of three. Defensemen are divided into pairs. The first group, X_1's, start drill with a rush. When they pass the blue line, the second group, X_2's, start a rush the other way. Defensive pairs react accordingly.

Tempo:

Drill is executed at full speed.

Participation:

The entire team.

1–1 Both Ways

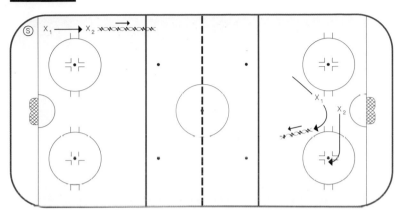

Purpose:

To provide a drill for 1 1 with constant movement.

Description:

Performed with two players making 1–1 rush. After first rush, they switch roles and make a 1–1 rush the other way.

Tempo:

Drill is executed at full speed.

Participation:

The entire team. Up to four rushes can be in progress simultaneously.

Variations:

Insert a third player for 2–1 drill.

DRILL
190 2–1 With Backchecker Both Ways

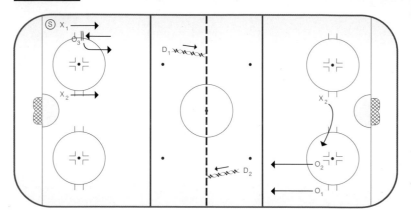

Purpose:
To provide a drill for a 2–1 where an offensive forward has to make the transition to defense.

Description:
Two forwards (X_1 and X_2) make a rush against the backchecker (O_3), and the defenseman (D). One of the forwards, X_2, becomes the backchecker in a 2–1 rush the other way led by O_1 and O_2.

Tempo:
Drill is executed at full speed.

Participation:
The entire team.

Variations:
D_1 can make the breakout pass for the second rush.

2–1 Both Ways

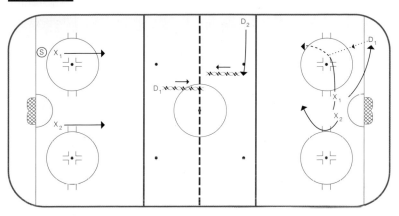

Purpose:

To provide a 2–1 drill that has the forwards make two rushes.

Description:

Two forwards (X_1 and X_2) make a 2–1 rush against the defenseman (D_1). A second rush is made the other way with D_1 making the breakout pass. D_2 would make the breakout pass if a third rush were added.

Tempo:

Drill is executed at full speed.

Participation:

The entire team.

2-1/3-1 With Backchecker

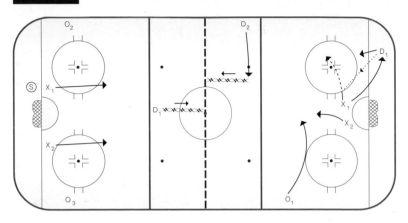

Purpose:

To provide a 2–1/3–1 drill with a backchecker.

Description:

The drill is the same as Drill 191 with the addition of a
backchecker. The backchecker (O_1) picks up one of the
forwards. A third forward added makes it a 3–1 drill with a
backchecker.

Tempo:

Drill is executed at full speed.

Participation:

The entire team.

3–2 Both Ways

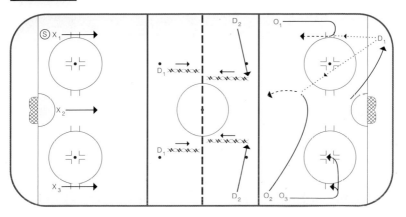

Purpose:

To provide a 3–2 drill with constant motion both ways.

Description:

Three forwards (X_1, X_2 and X_3) make a rush against the defensive pair (D_1's). At the completion of the rush, one of the defensemen (D_1) makes the breakout pass for the second group of forwards (O_1, O_2 and O_3). Another defensive pair (D_2's) are in the second rush.

Tempo:

Drill is executed at full speed.

Participation:

The entire team.

3-2/4-1

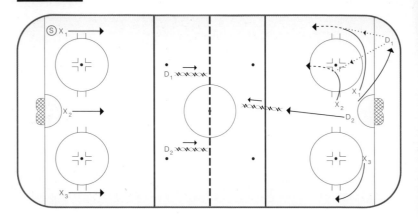

Purpose:

To provide a transition drill for the defensemen in a 3–2/4–1 rush.

Description:

Performed with three forwards (X_1, X_2 and X_3) making a rush against two defensemen (D_1 and D_2). After the initial rush, D_1 makes the breakout pass to the X's and joins them in a 4–1 rush against the other defenseman (D_2).

Tempo:

Drill is executed at full speed.

Participation:

The entire team.

Variations:

Add a defensive forward to make drill 3–3/4–2.

DRILL 195 3-2/5-2

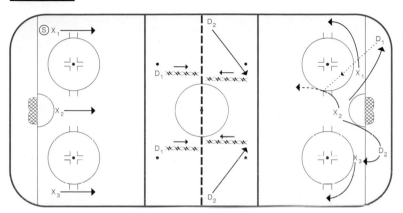

Purpose:
To provide a drill for a 3–2/5–2 with constant movement.

Description:
Performed with three forwards (X_1, X_2 and X_3) making a 3–2 rush against the defensive pair (D_1's). After the initial rush, a second rush is made 5–2 with the D_1's and the X's against the defensive pair (D_2's). D_1 makes the outlet pass on 5–2.

Tempo:
Drill is executed at full speed.

Participation:
The entire team.

Variations:
Add a defensive forward to make drill 3–3/5–3.

1-1 Game

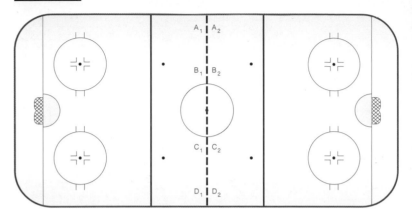

Purpose:

To provide a drill for a competitive game.

Description:

Multiple pairs are on the ice. Each pair plays a 1-1 game, i.e., A_1 vs. A_2. Winners play against winners.

Tempo:

Drill is executed at full speed.

Participation:

The entire team, up to five games of 1-1 can be played simultaneously.

Empty Net Game

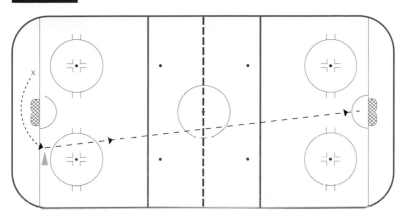

Purpose:

To provide a drill for a relaxed game.

Description:

Players skate around the net and shoot the puck at the empty net at the other end. Puck must be shot before shooter gets to face-off circle. Game continues until only one player is left.

Tempo:

Drill is executed at 3/4 speed.

Participation:

The entire team.

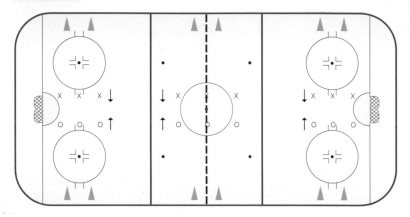

Purpose:

To provide a drill for a competitive game of 3–3.

Description:

Teams of three players play against each other. Games are played in all three zones. This means that up to 18 players can play simultaneously.

Tempo:

Drill is executed at 3/4 to full speed.

Participation:

The entire team.

Games of 4-4

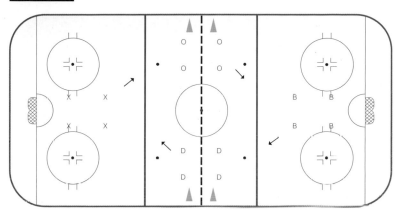

Purpose:

To provide a drill for a competitive game of 4-4.

Description:

Team is divided into groups of four. Each team, X's, O's, B's, and D's, have a net to defend and a net to score in. This means 16 players can play simultaneously.

Tempo:

Drill is executed at 3/4 to full speed.

Participation:

The entire team.

200 Full Squad Game

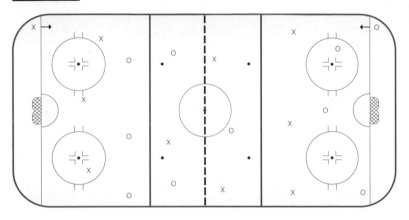

Purpose:

To provide a drill for a competitive game utilizing the entire team.

Description:

Team is divided into two squads, X's and O's. Each team has defenders, mid-fielders and scorers. The players cannot leave their appropriate zones. The puck has to move from zone to zone, i.e., defenders to mid-fielders to scorers. Keep score.

Tempo:

Drill is executed at full speed.

Participation:

The entire team.

Variations:

Have up to three pucks in play at once.

CHAPTER 9

Practice

"Every drill has its purpose. Not only are they devised to improve general condition, but also improve some basic fundamentals of the game."

John Wooden
They Call Me Coach

"The results of training depend on good organization. However, to no less degree do they depend on the proper methods which the coach employs, not only in selecting, but also conducting each drill or lesson on the whole."

Anatoli Tarasov
Road To Olympus

A good hockey team will be a good practice team; the same for a coach and the coaching staff — a good game coach needs to be a good practice coach. The coaching staff must put both time and effort into the practices for them to be fruitful.

Every coach must ask himself or herself, "How can I get the maximum use of the facility with the maximum amount of participation of the players to accomplish the objectives of the practice?" This question can only be answered and then implemented by putting time and effort into the design of the practice.

Coaches should not hesitate to use new and innovative ideas in their practices. Other sports can provide different ideas that are counter, but productive, to the traditional North American methods. Practices should not be with one coach, a lot of scrimmaging, a few drills and plenty of ice not being utilized.

Here are some suggestions to be considered when planning practices:

1. The one coach system should, if possible, be abandoned. It is not possible for one coach to effectively train, develop and teach 15-22 players simultaneously on the ice.
2. Define the objectives of each practice. Outline what should be accomplished in terms of skill development conditioning and tactics.
3. What are the capabilities of the players? The content of the practices need to complement their ability levels.
4. Decide how best to implement the objectives: what drills are to be used, how much time, if any, should be spent scrimmaging and how should the conditioning aspect be accomplished.
5. Specify how much time is to be spent on each part of practice. Once the time specifics are determined, they should be maintained.

6. Following each practice, the coaches should review the practice, evaluate its strengths and weaknesses and make suggestions on how to make improvements for future practices.
7. Keep practices from being boring. Boredom creates an atmosphere inconducive to learning.
8. Keep a record of all practices. They will be useful for future reference.

Year-long Plan

The coaching staff needs to have an idea of what has to be accomplished over the year. Prior to the start of the season, a year- (season) long plan should be completed. This plan should outline the development of the team and its individual members for the year.

What should be included in the year-long plan? First, the progress of the team, both technically and tactically, needs to be projected. This, in part, determines the approach to teaching the team's systems. It also determines the types of drills used and which skills to emphasize at different times. The plan helps the coaching staff stay calm and focused when the team is in a slump, or things are just not going well. Second, the progress of the individual players needs to be established and monitored. The plan takes into consideration how to improve and develop the players' skills while simultaneously focusing on team development.

Drill Selection

1. Select drills that complement the team's level of ability. Do not use drills that are too difficult or complex for the team's present ability level.
2. Select drills that utilize the entire, or as near as possible, ice surface. This can be done with one or a group of drills being executed at different spots simultaneously.

3. Select drills that utilize as many players as possible. It is important to keep the players active throughout the practice.
4. Select drills that complement the team's system of play.
5. Run drills in a time span that allows for the purpose of the drill to be accomplished and does not allow for players to become listless or bored.
6. All drills are fundamental. Keep in mind that drills to teach the basic fundamentals are always useful. No team ever progresses beyond the need for fundamental drills. There is no such thing as a drill being too basic or too simple.
7. Consider whether your team likes a large number of drills, or just a few drills. Each team has a distinct personality. Some teams like a large number of drills. Other teams are more comfortable with only a few familiar drills.

The following example practices are comprised of four components: skills (S), tactics (T), conditioning (C) and fun competition (F). They are 60 minutes in length. Each practice has a specific theme or focus.

Example Practices

---- ▮ ----

Minute 0–5: Warm-ups (S)

Light skating, doing turns, spins, falls, etc., with and without pucks.

Minute 6–15: Skill drills (S)

Three drills, one in each zone. (A) Backward skating on a face-off circle. (B) Players skate a figure 8 while stickhandling. (C) Standing still on a face-off circle, players make passes.

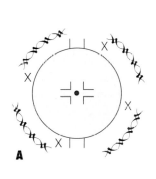

A

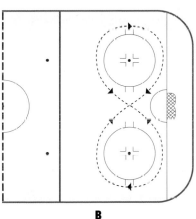

B

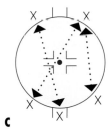

C

Minute 16–30: Breakout drills (T)

1 on 1's, 2 on 1's, 3 on 2's. Defenseman begins drill with an outlet pass.

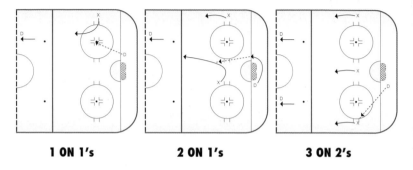

1 ON 1's   **2 ON 1's**   **3 ON 2's**

Minute 31–35: Conditioning drill (C)

Players skate one-and-a-half laps. Skate 22 sec., rest 44 sec. 3 times.

Minute 36–40: Passing drill (S)

Pairs make one-touch passes while moving in one zone.

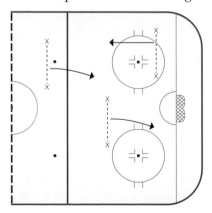

Minute 41–50: Forechecking (T)

Instruction on forechecking system. Players go through the system, as well as possible adjustments for the upcoming opposition.

Minute 51–55: Conditioning drill (C)

Players skate hard to the blue line, turn and come back to the goal line easy. Skate 4 sec./rest 12 sec. 6–8 times.

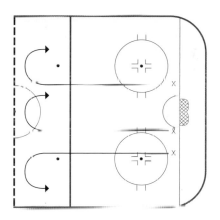

Minute 56–60: Relay race (F)

Teams of four players each, down and back once.

———————————— II ————————————

Minute 0–5: Warm-ups (S)

Skating easy, players in groups of three pass the puck between themselves. One player skates backward, two forward.

Minute 6–15: Shooting drills (S)

Two shooting drills, one in each end. (A) Player breaks off wing and shoots. (B) Forward passes to defenseman, breaks to the net, receives a return pass and shoots.

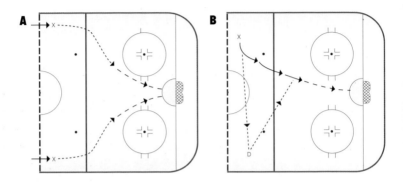

Minute 16–22: Defensive zone coverage (T)

Instruction on defensive zone coverage.

Minute 23–28: Counter-attack (T)

Three forwards begin 3 on 2 attack with outlet pass from a defenseman. Drill goes both ways.

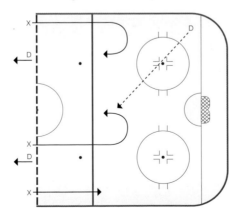

Minute 29–35: Conditioning drill (C)

Players skate down and back. Skate 15 sec./rest 45 sec. 5 times.

Minute 36–40: Stickhandling drill (S)

Players skate laps and (A) weave around cones, (B) make circles around cones and (C) stop at cones.

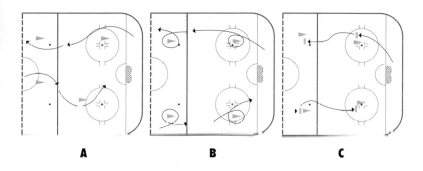

A   **B**   **C**

Minute 41–55: Power play and penalty killing (T)

Instruction and execution of power play and penalty killing situations.

Minute 56–60: Target shooting (F)

From the blue line, players try to hit frisbee that is hanging from the net.

Minute 0–5: Warm-ups (S)

Skating easy in pairs, players pass the puck between themselves and then play one on one. Executed while skating laps.

Minute 6–10: Shooting drill (S)

Players swing out of the corners and shoot on the goal.

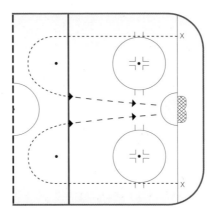

Minute 11–20: Passing drills (S)

Two drills executed on face-off circle. (A) Stationary passing and (B) While skating, make pass to player ahead.

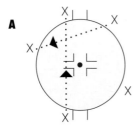

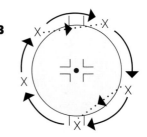

Minute 21–27: Neutral zone counter-attack (T)

Instruction on the neutral zone counter-attack.

Minute 28–35: Conditioning drill (C)

Skate width of the ice, over and back. Skate 15 sec./rest 45 sec. 5 times.

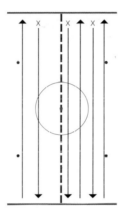

Minute 36–43: Puckhandling drill (S)

Players work on taking a pass in the feet and deflecting the puck to the stick.

Minute 44–50: Stickhandling drill (S)

Players working in pairs begin passing the puck between themselves. On whistle, they play 1 on 1 trying to keep the puck to themselves.

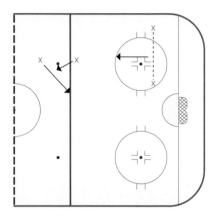

Minute 51–55: Shooting drill (S)

One player moves to the corner with a puck. Second player moves to the slot area and shoots or deflects a pass from the first player.

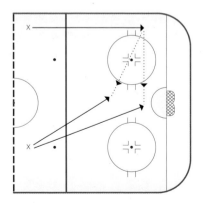

Minute 56–60: Rapid shooting (F)

Each player shoots five pucks quickly from the red line at the empty goal.

———————————————— **IV** ————————————————

Minute 0–5: Warm-ups (S)

Start with light, easy skating and gradually pick up the tempo.

Minute 6–10: Stickhandling drill (S)

Players, in groups of four or five, while carrying the puck, skate around each face-off circle.

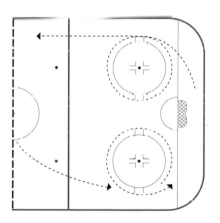

Minute 11–25: Skill drills (S)

(A) Player moves with the puck from the corner toward the net or the slot area. (B) Two players skate up ice making short passes and come back wide, each carrying a puck. (C) The players each have a puck and try to avoid each other.

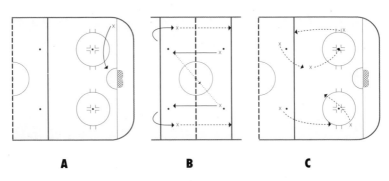

A　　　　　　**B**　　　　　　**C**

Minute 26–30: Face-offs (T)

Instructions on face-offs.

Minute 31–40: Conditioning drill (C)

Players in groups of four or five, skate two laps. Skate 30 sec./rest 90 sec. 4 times.

Minute 41–50: Power play and penalty killing (T)

Using units, both the power play and penalty kill situations are practiced.

Minute 51–60: Games of 3 on 3 (F)

Using the width of the ice, three separate games of 3 on 3 are played. Emphasize quick, short passes.

Minute 0–5: Warm-ups (S)

Easy skating and stretching, skate three laps each at a quicker tempo.

Minute 6–15: Skating drills (S)

Two drills. (A) Players skate to the red line, stop, take two or three quick strides in the other direction. (B) Work on forward and backward crossovers while skating on a face-off circle.

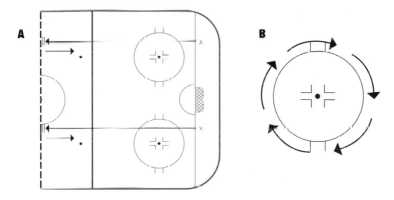

Minute 16–25: Aerobic skate (C)

Players skate at 60%–70% maximum continuously in laps. Skate 3 min./rest 1 min. 2 times.

Minute 26–40: Forechecking and breakouts (T)

Working with two units in each end, practice forechecking systems and breakout plays.

Minute 41–50: Skill drills (S)

Three drills. (A) Players work on taking a pass off the boards. (B) Players work on turns by skating figure 8's—going hard on turns and easy on straightaways. (C) Shooting drill has player receive a pass as the player moves into slot area and shoots.

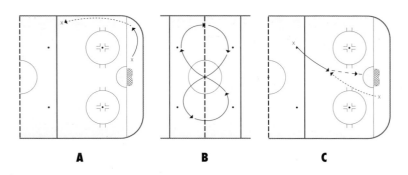

A   B   C

Minute 51–55: Conditioning drill (C)

Players work short, quick intervals by skating hard while carrying a puck. Skate 5 sec./rest 20 sec. 8 times.

Minute 56–60: Showdown (F)

Players engage in a simple penalty-shot drill. Winners advance until there is only one player left.

Minute 0–5: Warm-ups (S)

Easy skating with players working in pairs shadowing each other.

Minute 6–10: Shooting drill (S)

Players come off boards and shoot.

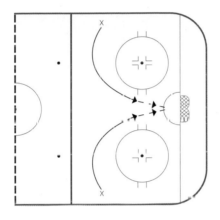

Minute 11–20: Checking (T)

(A) Centers and defensemen work on coverage in the net and the slot area. (B) Wings work on covering checks while backchecking.

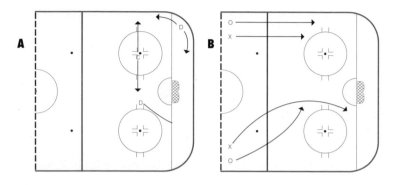

Minute 21–35: Conditioning drill (C)

Players skate three laps. Skate 60 sec./rest 180 sec. 3 times.

Minute 36–46: Skating drills (S)

Two skating drills. (A) Players work on stepovers. (B) Agility training with players moving in all four directions.

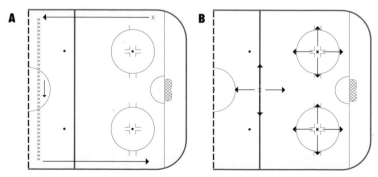

Minute 47–50: Breakout play (T)

Units breakout 5 on 2 to neutral zone, regroup and breakout a second time. Work both ends.

Minute 51–55: Conditioning drill (C)

Players skate between red line and blue line continuously. Skate 15 sec./rest 45 sec. 4 times.

Minute 56–60: Agility test (F)

Players are timed while skating an agility course.